A MYSTERY TO BE LIVED

A MYSTERY TO BE LIVED

JIM WILLIS

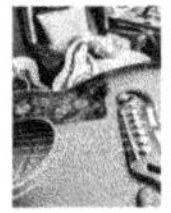

Other Books by Jim Willis

The Long Pivot Home: Based on a true story of love and loss in Oklahoma (ArtStrings Press, 2024).

Tinkertown: A Wheatfield, an Airbase, and Us (ArtStrings Press, 2024.)

The 1960s in Film (Santa Barbara: ABC-CLIO, 2021)

Daily Life in the 1960s Counterculture (Santa Barbara: ABC-CLIO, 2019).

Tweeting to Freedom, (Santa Barbara, ABC-CLIO, 2017).

Documents Decoded: 1960s Counterculture, (Santa Barbara: ABC-CLIO, 2015).

From Twitter to Tahrir Square: Ethics of Social and New Media Communications, (Santa Barbara: Praeger, 2014.)

Daily Life Behind the Iron Curtain (Santa Barbara: Greenwood Press, 2013).

100 Media Moments That Changed America (Santa Barbara: Greenwood), December, 2009.

The Mind of a Journalist: How Reporters View Themselves, Their Craft, and Their World (Thousand Oaks: Sage, 2009).

The Media Effect: How the News Influences Politics and Government (Santa Barbara:Praeger,), 2007.

The Human Journalist: Reporters, Perspectives and Emotions, (Westport: Praeger) 2003.

Prelude to Greatness: Sooner Football in the 1990s, with Jay Smith (Norman: University of Oklahoma Press), 2003.

Images of Germany in the American Media (Westport: Praeger, 1997).

Reporting on Risks: The Practice and Ethics of Health Reporting, with Albert Okunade (Santa Barbara: Praeger, 1996.)

The Age of Multimedia and Turbonews (Santa Barbara: Praeger, 1993).

New Directions in Media Management, with Diane Willis (Boston:Allyn & Bacon, 1992).

The Shadow World: Life Between the News Media and Reality (Santa Barbara:Praeger, 1991).

Journalism: State of the Art (Santa Barbara: Praeger, 1990).

Surviving in the Newspaper Business: Newspaper Management in Turbulent Times, (Santa Barbara: Praeger, 1988).

Praise for
"Tinkertown"

One of the author's latest books is **Tinkertown: A Wheatfield, an Airbase, and Us,** published in 2024. Here is a sampling of reviews about that book:

"*Tinkertown* is a rich, exciting history which deserves to be read, and remembered, not for just the planes and their dramatic missions, but for the hearty men and women who came here to build them, and along the way, created a community which still flourishes today. Especially compelling are Willis' stories told by workers at Tinker AFB. It's stories like these that make *Tinkertown* an important book, and a reminder of what was achieved in the past by people collaborating together to work for a common goal." -- Pam Olson, *The Oklahoman.*

"Jim Willis has been writing about the society around him for several decades, but *Tinkertown* may be his most impactful and certainly the most personal effort to date. As Jim shared his experiences in Midwest City, my own memories kicked in and it became personal for me as well. What we learn about the value of looking outward from ourselves to the betterment and service of others is transcendent and worth our attention."-- From the Foreword to *Tinkertown* by Gen. Roger A. Brady, (Ret.) USAF.

"I'm a former librarian who has read numerous local histories and memoirs, most of which were not very good, so this book came as a lovely surprise. It is so well written and researched that the pages almost turn themselves. I grew up in Midwest City and worked summers at Tinker AFB and knew quite a bit of history of the area but I learned so much more from this book. Dr. Willis manages to weave his personal memories with the facts to make an entertaining read." -- Jan Smith

VIII ~

About this Book

Since writing *Tinkertown: A Wheatfield, an Airbase, and Us,* I have wanted to add to that book's theme of life's influences on who we are as individuals. That book's focus is on the question, *how much of me is where I'm from?* I thought, what if my *next* book could focus *mostly* on the related question, *how much of me is what I've witnessed and done **since then?*** (A caveat: I knew I couldn't resist the temptation to drop in a few stories from childhood, too, though.)

Enter, *A Mystery to be Lived: An Oklahoma Writer's Stories of Life and Love.* This book walks the reader through life's experiences that are sometimes wonderful, sometimes sad, sometimes tragic, and often something in-between; even very humorous. It is a kind of puzzle that asks to be solved. Indeed, one of the stories in this book compares a part of our lives to the Rubik's Cube.

But therein lies the rub: Life's mysteries are sometimes *unsolvable.* They just must be lived, and they offer rich memories and lessons to be learned. Indeed, the book's title is a phrase that comes from the 19th century philosopher Soren Kierkegaard who said, *"Life is a mystery to be lived; not a problem to be solved."* I like that because it puts the focus on the living and not just on trying to figure life out. We do enough of the latter already, but we don't do that much of the former. The thing is, we must first *live* our lives in order to *understand* them.

A Mystery to be Lived is a series of nearly 50 personal narratives the author has lived and/or reported on as a career journalist, author, urban cowboy, and college professor. That is what might interest you in a book about life from a guy you probably don't know, who is from Oklahoma, and who now lives in Kentucky with his beloved wife and adopted family of six wayward and wonderful animals. (Not to mention our kids and grandkids, of course!)

So, here are some more specifics to entice you to read on:

- These are all short, stand-alone stories about life's emotions we've all felt, so you will probably find your own familiar emotions and memories within them. Our pasts may be different, but I'll bet what we've learned and felt is similar.
- You can read them in any order (although 13-18 are closely related), pop out and pop in as you like, or (probably) find it a page-turner that won't let you put it down!
- I tell stories of my life around the world. Here are a few places I've lived and/or worked: Boston, Los Angeles, Dallas, Memphis, St. Louis, and Indianapolis. That's just in this country. I've also worked internationally in Berlin, Frankfurt, Dresden, Moscow, Novosibirsk (Siberia), Barcelona, Cologne, London, New Delhi, Agra, Chandigarh, Jaipur, Paris, Tokyo, Bangkok, Seoul, and even in the Latvian capital of Riga (which rivals Alaska for late-night sun and makes great bagels).
- You can't help but see a lot of life, and from different perspectives, when you do that kind of business travel.
- My business is fact-gathering and reporting, which are what we used to call "journalism" before that word got smeared by the extremist ideologues on the political scale. It's most noticeable on the far right, but some is there on the far left, too.
- I've reported on some of the biggest stories in the world, such as the 1995 Oklahoma City bombing, the fall of the Berlin Wall and its anniversaries, what everyday life was like behind the Iron Curtain before that Wall fell in 1989, and how Germany handled the influx of a million Syrian refugees in 2014 and 2015.
- If you scan the Table of Contents for *A Mystery to be Lived*, you will find some of these story topics listed there. But you might scratch your head when you come across stories like, "If I'm Ever Abducted, Arrest my Guitar," or "Hayley Mills, Me, and the Skytrain Theater," or "Mad Max, my Hernia, and Me." So, read on to the next point, to wit:

- Sometime after I grew tired of searching for life by keeping the airlines in business as a Platinum Plus passenger, I decided to write about the life I have lived, no matter where I was living it. I realized that some of the deepest influences on me occurred right in my home state of Oklahoma and my unique hometown of Midwest City, Oklahoma. After all, it was there that I developed my passion for reading from my Dad, my love of teaching from my mom, my understanding of loyalty from my sister, and my fiery desire to become a writer from the Midwest City Library books I read.

- Some of the things I've witnessed have been immensely joyous. Some have been disappointments. Some have been in-between, and some have been absolutely horrible. Each has influenced me, and each has taught me lessons about life and about love.

- You'll see a lot about *dreams and dreaming* in these pages, too. That's not accidental, because I've always been a dreamer.

- In my later years, I have come to a point of embracing the mysteries of life, and I suppose I'll feel that way at least until the next horrible thing might happen, either to me or others I care about. And yet, after those sad moments pass in the future, I'll no doubt be glad for experiencing them. What's the phrase? *That which doesn't kill you, makes you stronger.* So, if I'm dead, I won't care; if I'm still alive, I'll be stronger.

- A guy I quote so much that his words have become my mantra is the fictional Tom Wingo, chief protagonist in Pat Conroy's *The Prince of Tides.* A fine film version of that book was made into a movie of the same name in the 1980s. I write about it in this book. But one of Wingo's last lines has stayed with me now for 40 years. He's out mowing his high school football field when he says, "It is the mystery of life that sustains me now. I am a teacher, a coach, and a well-loved man, and that is *more* than enough." It is for me, too.

• Oh, one final reason you might want to give my book a try: It is my 23rd so far, and I think I've finally gotten the hang of putting readable pages between the front and back covers. Most of the chapters in this book are written specifically for it. But a few sneaked in from previous books, blogs, and submissions to the MyRetrospect.com writer's site. That's the site and the group that finally convinced me that, after a life of writing about others, it's okay to shoot a selfie sometimes. I suppose this book is a selfie, but one with universal resonance. I hope you enjoy and find personal meaning in *A Mystery to be Lived*. I'm convinced that, while our experiences may be different, they are very similar in the emotions they provoke, and in the lessons they teach. Happy reading!

-- Jim Willis

Into the Unknown

"You move in mysterious ways, Lord." -- William Cowper, 1773
"Life is a Mystery to be Lived; not a problem to be solved."
-- Soren Kierkegaard, circa 1845

Contents

Other Books by Jim Willis · v
Praise for "Tinkertown" · vii
About this Book · ix
Into the Unknown · xiii
Dedication · xiv

1 You'll Never Know Until You Go · 1
2 Gridirons and Goat Heads · 8
3 If I'm Ever Abducted, Arrest my Guitar · 15
4 Mad Max, My Hernia, and Me · 19
5 Summer Memories · 25
6 We Were Not All Cowboys · 28
7 Hayley Mills, Me, and the Skytrain Theater · 33
8 First Wheels of Freedom · 37
9 Whatever Happened to Kid TV? · 40
10 Memories of my Dad · 44
11 Scouting in the Buff · 49
12 At Dawn, We Attack! · 53
13 My Year as a Bandit · 57
14 A Town Called Erick · 61
15 Can We Go Home Again? · 66

16 A Day Unlike Any Other   71

17 A Play Drive and a Prey Drive   77

18 A Horse Named Star   82

19 A Farewell in Oklahoma City   87

20 The "Home" in Oklahoma   101

21 Last Night I Had the Strangest Dream   104

22 Feeling Whole Again in Oklahoma City   110

23 When Your World Expands, Embrace It   114

24 Germans Celebrate 25 Years of Freedom   124

25 Immigrants, Germany and Luther   132

26 Me, I've Lived in Dreams   141

27 Perchance Not to Dream   144

28 Love at First Sight   148

29 Checking Out of Hotel Reno   153

30 The Win-Win of Homestay Parenthood   161

31 A Dress Rehearsal for Life   166

32 Those Magical Musicals   170

33 A Moment of His Own   174

34 Tom Wingo, Dr. Sandhu, and Me   177

35 OU Football, Jay, and Me   182

36 You're a Good Man, C.B.!   187

37 I Miss the Unity that Came with the News   191

38 The Big Sister Factor   196

39 The Song(?) Remembers When   199

40 Washday Miracle in Stillwater   202

41 A Distant Trumpet   206

42 Cupid on the Keys   216

43 The Furry Feud   223

44 My Rubik's Cube of Religion 228

45 Answering my own Question 235

46 We Lions in Winter 240

47 Like a Circle in a Spiral 244

About the Author 249

1

You'll Never Know Until You Go

It was interesting to lecture about press freedom at the University of Moscow, right across the street from Red Square.

Olga Kravtsova

Ever since I was a kid, I always dreamed about being someplace else. All my life I've dealt with wanderlust, and I have spent time feeling guilty about it until I finally came to peace with it a few years back.

Over the years I've admired friends who stayed home and built something, like George Bailey in *It's a Wonderful Life*. Instead, I've been like George's brother Harry who left home and family for other adventures.

It wasn't that I had an unhappy home life; it was great and I felt secure in my parents' love. And it wasn't that we lived in a rundown shack with a leaky roof. Ours was a small middle-class home in the new town of Midwest City, Oklahoma, and my sister and I each had our own bedrooms. It was fine.

Still, all this satisfaction lived alongside my wanderlust, and it was my unbounded imagination — often unleashed in the Narnia of my own bedroom — that allowed me to go places and experience adventures. They may have been virtual trips, but they were better than anything Oculus has produced in the VR age.

Case in point: my dad's catalogues from the Alaska Sleeping Bag Company. This was a now-defunct outdoor outfitters company that fell to the other giants of Eddie Bauer, Orvis, and L.L. Bean. But in the sixties, it was king.

Every few months, this book would arrive in our mailbox, and my dad (apparently with his own case of wanderlust) would devour it and then turn it over to me. The company's narrow name belied the fact that it featured so much more than sleeping bags. Inside were page after page of everything a hearty soul might need to live and survive an outdoor adventure in the Alaskan wilds. All manner of camping gear, clothing, survival gear, rifles, bows, and arrows ... the works.

What could be better than grabbing my dog Laddie, packing up all my neat gear from the Alaska Sleeping Bag Co., and heading off to the Klondike? It was the stuff my dreams were made of, and there were plenty of those dreams.

So it was that *travel* became my lifelong guilty pleasure.

From virtual to real

When I got my driver's license and went to college, my virtual trips began turning into real travels. Before I graduated, I had crisscrossed the Southwest three times, from Oklahoma to California and back, either by car, plane, or bus. Route 66 (both the old and new versions) was becoming my new best friend, and those road trips would prove to be only the precursors of countless more in the future.

That would be particularly true during my marital commuter years when I worked in L.A. and my wife Annie worked in Ohio. I got to know every wide spot in the road intimately. I considered having "Route 66" tattooed across my chest but opted instead for a good t-shirt saying the same thing. I still toy with the idea of asking Annie to scatter my ashes out on a stretch of the Mother Road in New Mexico.

New York, New York

I was teaching at the University of Missouri in 1978, when I agreed to drive eleven journalism students to a Society of Professional Journalists convention in New York City in a 12-passenger van. We were all excited about rubbing shoulders with A-list journalists and hearing from the bow-tied iconoclast Charles Osgood: the man CBS called the poet-laureate of radio news.

Our expectations were all exceeded, although the road trip itself hinted at disaster more than once. It doesn't take much imagination to realize what could go wrong with a mini-busload of 20-year-olds, especially when the spirited coeds in the group decided to strike up flirtatious chats over the CB radio with passing truckers, some of whom we'd run into at a couple truck stops down the line.

There's a *Halloween* movie in there somewhere.

About the City itself, New York was the first of my future destinations to send a jolt of electricity through every fiber of my being. Rubbernecking with my students out on Broadway, late at night after an out-of-body experience called *A Chorus Line*, I felt my life had just begun at age 32.

If I hadn't already become hooked on traveling, I was on this night.

The last place on earth

I was on assignment covering the one-year anniversary of the aptly named Bhopal Disaster in India, which occurred on Dec. 2, 1984, when a Union Carbide pesticide plant exploded, sending toxic fumes into the air and killing upwards to 8,000 people and injuring another half-million. I was doing a story for *Nieman Reports*, the Harvard-based publication for the Nieman Foundation which honors top journalists.

I was asked to interview journalists around India on how that disaster was covered. Part of my journey took me into Sikh regions where violent outbreaks had occurred, and I discovered halfway through my three-week trip that the Indian government was tracking me. I never found out why, although some people I encountered thought I was with the CIA.

Apparently, they weren't the only ones thinking that. One night in Chandigarh I was asked to talk to about a hundred Indian journalists about journalism in America. I sensed a tension in the large room when the evening began, and I assumed it had something to do with the Sikh/Hindi civil war in the region. About halfway through my talk, I started asking the crowd questions about how free they felt to report news about their government. Without warning, an angry man jumped up from his seat in the front row, charged my podium, shoved me out of the way, grabbed my notes, and sped off toward the exit.

It all happened so fast, I was stunned. A silence settled over the room, and I continued with my talk. Meanwhile, my Sikh host and a couple other men gave chase to the man who stole my notes. They were returned to me after my talk with profuse apologies and the explanation, "When you started asking questions, Dr. Willis, he thought you sounded like a CIA agent. Press freedom in this part of the country is questionable, and some journalists here are worried about government spying and crackdowns. I'm so sorry."

I assured him I was all right, and I realized later at the hotel that I learned something valuable that night: I should be more aware of the conditions of the country I'm addressing.

This lesson would be helpful years later when I was lecturing on press freedom in Russia, a country not known for that privilege. It was also helpful when I spoke in the Basque region of Spain. It was there I chose to talk about *terrorism*, since I had just recently covered the Oklahoma City bombing. But, when my Spanish government handlers, asked me beforehand about my topic, they sensed danger. "You know, Dr. Willis, this region of Spain is in civil unrest, and we've had terrorist incidents, too. Some of the people who hear you may be Separatists themselves." I did continue with the topic, but I did soft-pedal my use of the word "terrorism."

Shimla, India

One of my stops took me on a treacherous train and bus ride into the northern mountain city of Shimla, nestled into the foothills of the Himalayas. I vividly recall thinking, as our bus driver was making harrowing hairpin turns a few thousand feet up, that this might be one trip I'd never return from. I was able to catch my breath for only a minute when our bus arrived in Shimla near midnight.

As the overhead lights went on in our packed bus, we were mobbed by a horde of hungry hands and arms lowering our windows and reaching inside for any handouts we might have. Then the driver opened the door, and we were thrust out into this throng to fend for ourselves. Fortunately, the natives were friendly, and we wound up enjoying ourselves immensely over the next few days, which happened to be Christmas Week.

Riding a yak up a mountain trail proved interesting, as did sharing beers with three Russian soldiers in a pub on New Year's Eve.

Asian rendezvous x 2

In 1988 and 1992, I made two trips to Asia. The first was to Seoul to meet my first son, Min, and the second was to Bangkok to meet my second son, Kao.

We had adopted Min through an international agency and had cleared all the hurdles necessary to go get him in South Korea and, as a bonus, our weeklong visit in Seoul coincided with the Summer Olympics that city was hosting.

Count this as a double-barreled dose of guilty pleasure.

I made the Bangkok trip alone because I was uncertain how it would play out. We were not working through an agency but instead were taking a calculated risk in working with a doctor who was having luck smuggling orphans out of the ravages of Cambodia to better lives in the West. This trip, and the eventual midnight handoff of Kao to me in neighboring Thailand at a place aptly named Hotel Reno, would take too long to relate here. But it was successful and a trip I will never forget. I write more about them both, once in verse and once in prose in later chapters of this book.

To the Wall

Shortly after the publication of a 1994 book I wrote called, *The Age of Multimedia and TurboNews*, I received a letter from the U.S. State Department asking if I would be up for conducting a weeklong lecture tour of German universities on the book. I agreed and soon was on my way to Frankfurt and cities beyond for my first look at Deustschland. Happily, it would not be my last, as I've been asked back for numerous other lecture tours there and in other parts of Europe as well.

These trips morphed into freelance reporting assignments covering the 10th, 20th, and 25th anniversaries of the **Mauerfall** in Berlin, which had taken place the night of Nov. 9, 1989, and covering the Syrian refugee crisis in Germany in 2015. Altogether, there have been some 20 German trips with — hopefully — more to come.

The first time I toured the Checkpoint Charlie Museum and walked across the brick-path reminder of the Berlin Wall on Friedrichstrasse, I realized all people must have the universal hunger for freedom. Hundreds of East Germans were killed over 28 years trying to cross that dividing line between the former East and West Germany. Each time I cross the street now, I realize how precious freedom is and how much I take it for granted in America.

So, I often tell my students that I go to Berlin to remember and to get my freedom batteries recharged.

A few miles beyond that

It is 6,066 miles from L.A., where I was living in 2014, to Moscow. It is another 1,747 miles beyond Moscow to the city of Novosibirsk, which is in Siberia. That was my destination that winter and, in more than one way, it seemed a few miles past the last place on earth.

I was asked to deliver a week's worth of master lectures on American journalism at the University of Novosibirsk and later at the University of Moscow. I immediately began packing some thermal underwear and associated icebox-weather gear. Where was the Alaska Sleeping Bag Co. catalogue when I needed it? I then boarded a plane at an LAX terminal whose travel destination could have read *"The Ends of the Earth."*

I was eager to see if Russia measured up to the "Evil Empire" status that Ronald Reagan gave it in the 1980s. I'd always expected that was a bit of political hyperbole, and I was happy to find out I was right. Maybe I should hedge a bit by saying none of the people I encountered fit that moniker. What I *did* encounter was a lot of snow.

A *whole* lot of snow.

More importantly, in both Novosibirsk and Moscow, I found academic communities of dedicated and friendly scholars and students who were eager to see if I measured up to the "Evil Empire of the West" status that they had heard about. I also found two very good universities both eager to exchange scholars with America and to learn from each other.

Chalk Russia up as a guilty pleasure that I am still deconstructing.

The armchair view

Now, as a retiree twice-over, I presume I will be doing mostly armchair travel from now on. I could be wrong because the email stream between Germany and me is still active. If I am done, though, that's okay. Up to this moment, I realize I haven't really had time to go back in my mind and heart to savor what all these guilty pleasures have meant to me. This essay, in fact, is a good start.

Possibly the best way to sum all this up is to relate one of my favorite thoughts about the pleasure of travel. It comes from T.S. Eliot who said, *"Only those who risk going too far can possibly find out how far one can go."*

Come to think of it, I still haven't seen Alaska …

Gridirons and Goat Heads

Growing up in Oklahoma, I didn't know too many guys who weren't dreaming about being a star football player for the University of Oklahoma or Oklahoma State University. Bud Wilkinson was the legendary coach of the 1950s for the Sooners whose teams posted a miraculous 47-game winning streak between 1953 and 1957, before Notre Dame brought it to an end, 7-0, of that year.

Fall was for football in Oklahoma.
ArtTower/Pixabay

So yes, I was one of those dreamers, probably knowing all along it wouldn't come true. That didn't stop me from giving it a shot, starting at my Westside Elementary School. I reported for football practice in the early fall of 1958. Our head coach was Mr. Sales, and the assistant coach was Mr. Blackwell, both of them really nice men. Our practice field was just south of the school building and play-ground, across the parking lot. It was one of those fields that looked so huge when you were 11 years old, but which you thought was a postage stamp when you saw it in later years.

I remember two problems with that field, though, and the second one was especially irksome.

The first was the Dairy Queen over on the southwest corner of the field. The smells wafting over from its hamburgers, fries, and ice cream cones, were a real distraction from focusing on football. I often wondered if getting knocked around out here on the practice field and sweating my butt off was the best way to spend my afterschool time. How about just hanging out with a banana split at the DQ instead? On more than one of those daydream moments, Coach Sales' whistle would go off, and usually was directed at getting my attention.

"You want to play ball, Jimmy, or you want to go get a cone?" he would say.

Grown-ups shouldn't tempt a kid like that. But I opted for sweaty football, for whatever reason.

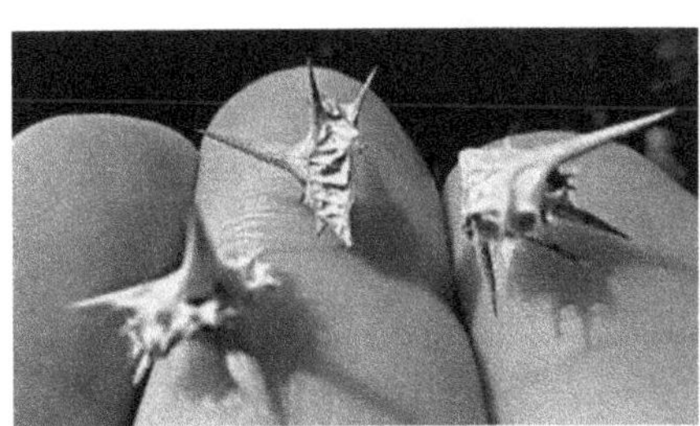

Goat Heads came with the gridirons.

The second distraction was/were the *Goat Heads*. Not as in actual farmyard animal heads, though. These were the infamous sticker balls that were so ubiquitous on the Oklahoma plains. They were like little cactus balls, only you didn't spot these before they landed in your skin. And since each individual spike grew out at different angles, there was no way to pull out one without watching another rip your skin at the same time.

For the lineman and occasional tight end that I was, there was no way I could stay off the ground. Nine out of 10 plays, I'd be picking myself up off the turf and pulling goat heads out of my arms while in the huddle. I came to love it when our running plays went through the other side of the line instead of my side. I would sometimes suggest that to our quarterback, even.

"Hey Johnny," I remember pleading in the huddle, "how about sending the ball through the *left tackle* this time? I'm bleeding goat heads over on my side!"

"No way, Jimmy!" he would respond. "You're the quickest guy we've got on the line, so we'll keep coming your way. The scoreboard shows it's working!"

I suppose it was about this time in life when I began to rate priorities. In this case, the main goal was to win the game, right? Coming my way seemed to help accomplish that. But was it worth all these bloody goat heads in my hands, arms, and legs?

But, since that's not the kind of discussion a guy can have with his brawny teammates, I always kept those Q&A sessions to myself.

I do remember talking it over once with my friend Max one time, though. He thought about it and then said, "Hey Jim, if you're gonna' help win one for the team, you gotta' go with *team* priorities. Even if your mom has to buy bigger boxes of bandages."

I guess I started getting used to sticker pain, because the goat heads bothered me a little less as the season wore on. Except when we played our crosstown rivals, Eastside Elementary, on their field. I was convinced *they* brought in extra buckets of goat heads and spread them in places on the field that they would know about but we wouldn't.

Later, as an adult living in Boston, I was told the Celtics did a similar thing with their parquet court in the old Boston Garden arena.

Here's how that worked, assuming the story is true:

The Boston Garden's parquet floor was known around the league for its unique square pattern. The court was made from scrap lumber, which created uneven bounces of the ball in some areas. Those were called "dead spots." A lot of players lost possession of the ball if it hit one of these spots. The court drew a lot of players' and coaches' complaints, saying it gave an unfair advantage to the team that knew where these dead spots were. That would be the home team Celtics. Sometimes they just didn't seem to be in the same places. There was a legend that grew as the seasons went on that the Celtics actually re-arranged some of the dead spot squares on purpose to give their team an advantage. Nevertheless, Celtics legends like Larry Bird and Danny Ainge denied that story.

Back to Oklahoma, I enjoyed playing football for the Westside Warriors and knew most of the players from my neighborhood. Our equipment was pretty basic, and some stuff didn't fit right, but it was just fine with us.

The late 50s were the time when face masks were being added to helmets, but only a few players wore them until the more durable ones came out. The earliest of them were made of cheap plastic, and I once remember seeing one of our opponents put his fist right through my teammate's mask. It broke right in half. Still, I was proud of having one of the first face masks on our team, even though it was just a single bar, and even though my dad had to buy it for me at the local sporting goods store. The school didn't supply them.

"Wow, Jimmy!" my coach said when he saw my new face mask. "How cool is that? You look like a real football player now!"

"Thanks, Coach," I said, silently wondering if I hadn't resembled a real football player during the games.

The problem with my whole headgear, however, was two-fold:

First, my helmet was a size too big, so it flopped around on my head a lot unless I stuffed a big rag in it. Even then, though, I would often pull myself up off the goat head field and find myself looking out my helmet's ear hole. At the beginning of this chapter, you'll find a Westside Warriors team picture. Even though we were standing perfectly still for the photo, my helmet is still slightly askew.

Second, my new face mask probably did save my two front teeth, but it only exacerbated the fact that my helmet was sitting ajar on my head, because the face bar was going sideways. I suppose, though, there was *some* safety in that whenever I was hit from the flank.

Third row up, third kid to the right of Coach Sales, before my face mask went on, but the helmet is still ajar.

Honest to God, with all the body slamming going on, there were times I'd stand up and not even know which end of the field our end zone was on. I do remember we won our share of games in my two years on the team, and I had a good time with the guys learning what teamwork was all about.

I took a break from the gridiron in my Jarman Junior High years and focused more on my newfound sports of swimming and diving. But when high school rolled around in 1960, I was ready to put on the pads again and see if there were fewer goat heads on the MCHS practice field. No such luck, so the battle continued and Mom kept buying more Band Aids. I liked our head coach at Midwest City High, Jim Darnell, and he was already on his way to becoming a legendary winner with his Bomber teams. But I still loved being in the pool more than on the practice field, so I turned in my pads.

Another reason for my decision, was I had developed a new hobby of photography by this time, and I enjoyed shooting pictures for the school paper, *The Bomber Beam*. But I couldn't both shoot the pictures and play at the same time, so I looked at my new 35mm camera and then looked at the goat head still in my arm from yesterday, and I chose the camera. Football would have to wait. That was fine with my folks, because they had already paid for enough dental work from damage my teeth had suffered on the field.

Still, toting a camera around wasn't as alluring to the girls at school as toting some kind of ball, so in my junior year I told our coach John Pratt that I'd like to try out for basketball. Turns out, though, I knew very little about the tactics and strategy of this game, and it always seemed to be more like semi-organized chaos on the court to me. I usually found myself in the wrong position at the wrong time, but I was just starting to get the hang of the game when I collided with the gym ceiling one day. I know, odd, right?

Coach Pratt had us run PT sprints up and down the long rows of risers, which worked okay until I turned my head to answer a question near the top bleacher when WHAM! My head slammed into the corner of one of the iron beams holding up the ceiling. I was out before the blood came spurting out of my skull, and when I awoke, I was headed to the hospital. A couple hours later, I was stitched up but in a wheelchair because my vertical balance was too rubbery to walk out of the hospital to Mom's car.

The next day, Coach Pratt came to see me at home and thanked me for my desire to play but said the school needed me to stay in one piece more than it needed me on the basketball court.

I got less sympathy from my girlfriend at the time whose nickname was "Tigger" and who liked to write out her thoughts in verse. This is the birthday card Tigger made me that referenced my short-lived basketball career:

"I used to think that folks who slammed into things like bleachers were clumsy, until I met the RISERS! Now, I'm CONVINCED! – Happy Birthday Old Man!!"

She finished it off with a cute little sketch of me lying prone on the court, leaking a pool of blood from my skull. I still have that card, and I sure did like Tigger, but we didn't date for long after that.

So much for war wounds wooing women.

My athletic attention went immediately back to the pool where, unless the diving board attacked me, I should be able to survive life on the swimming team. So it was that swimming, the thing I was best at, became my life sport. I still remember swimming in the State Finals Swim Meet at Douglas High School in Oklahoma City the spring of 1963.

That's another memory that refuses to wash off. It's the one sport I emerged from uninjured.

3

If I'm Ever Abducted, Arrest my Guitar

My guitar collection has grown from one to, well ...

Jim Willis

When I turned 14 years old, Dad gifted me with my very first guitar. The year was 1960, I was in the 8th grade at Jarman Junior High School in Midwest City, Oklahoma, and I was on the cusp of falling in love with folk music, via the Kingston Trio. Their ballad, *Tom Dooley* had just landed on the charts, and I was an instant fanThere was something about the blend of their guitars and voices that struck a chord deep inside me. It was like I just didn't *hear* their music; I *felt* it. I felt it very deeply. So much so, I made a vow to myself.

I was going to be a folk singer when I got my own guitar.

My first guitar

So, when I saw what my birthday present was, I was ecstatic. But when I first pressed the fingers of my left hand to its strings, I realized I had a problem. I had to press with all my digital strength just to touch those strings to the neck of that guitar. After just a couple minutes, those fingers became very sore and I had yet to produce a discernible chord.

What I didn't know, however, is that this was not all my fault. The guitar came from Sears and, although it was a Silvertone a respectable brand back then), it was an *archtop* guitar, and the action (the height of the strings from the neck) would have probably made even Chet Atkins angry. Today's luthiers do a much better job keeping that action low, but this was 65 years ago and this was an inexpensive Silvertone with very bad action.

I tried taking formal guitar lessons over at a guitar store on Air Depot Boulevard in my hometown of Midwest City, Oklahoma. But, like most structured music lessons, the instructor started with music theory, which I quickly grew tired of. I just wanted to learn enough chords to play some of the great folk ballads that were spewing out of gifted songwriters like Pete Seeger, Joni Mitchell, and a new guy named Bob Dylan.

Three chords and the truth, Man. That's all I wanted from Jenkins Music Store.

And maybe some softer guitar strings. My fingers' callouses were developing callouses.

Some Progress

I kept at it and made some forward movement, even on that Silvertone archtop. But it was slow, and I was questioning whether I had the DNA of a guitar player.

As she often did in crossroad moments, enter Mom. She was founder and principal of a curriculum-driven preschool she called Jack & Jill in Midwest City, and music education was an important part of that school. So she knew where to go for good instruments in

Oklahoma City. One of those places was Woodmansee-Abbott Music Co.

A Mom moment

Mom had seen my frustration with my Silvertone, so she took me up to this store one day. I was 17 and was thunderstruck by all the different kind of guitars there were. I thought the archtop design was the only guitar there was until I encountered the *flattop*. When I picked one up and started fingering it, I was amazed at how easy it was to play. The action was infinitely better than my Silvertone archtop, and I knew I'd found an instrument that I didn't have to fight anymore. I could just concentrate on learning my songs.

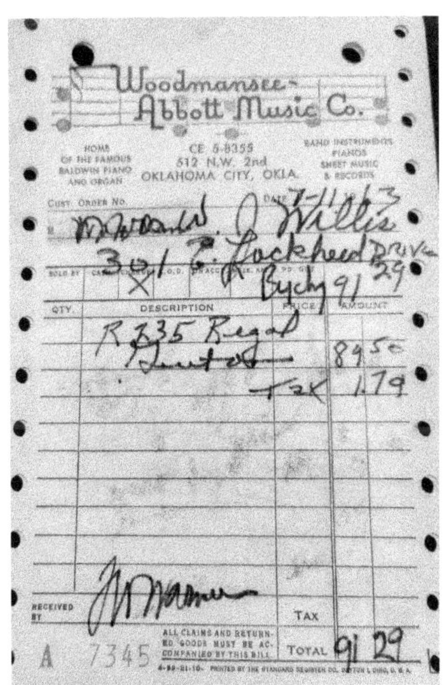

Mom's gift to me.

I still remember Mom instantly laying down the large sum of $91.29 for that guitar. In 1963 that was worth about $1,000 in today's world. She put it on an installment plan for about $30 per month, because she didn't have that much in the bank. She told me later she would have paid more, and done it quicker, if she'd known it would make me so happy.

Mom saw me through a lot during those teen years, but this spontaneous sacrifice she made is one of my most loving memories of her.

From that moment, I became inseparable from my guitar. I taught myself a lot, but a big break came when I met a church pastor in Oklahoma City who set up some informal one-on-one lessons with me and taught me how to use all of my guitar neck with what we call barre chords.

A personal instrument

I know the guitar fits the solitude I often prefer in life, as well as my introspective nature. Six decades later, I still sit alone in my study at night playing my guitar and singing the songs of my life's soundtrack. Jim's top hits. The list has changed, and the single guitar of my teens has morphed into eight, all of which adorn the walls and guitar stands around me.

Often I just lower the lights, sometimes I just use blue ambient lighting, and I get lost in my musical reverie.

I've worked through, and survived, many stressful times in life because of these late nights picking, strumming, singing, and even writing my own songs now and then. Technically, I'd still rate myself at only the intermediate level, with one caveat. My playing style is my own, and I've worked up some pretty unique playing patterns.

Stage fright

The thing is, even after playing for so many decades, I'm still nervous playing in front of anyone but my wife -- and my dogs of course. The latter actually seen spellbound by my music, and use it to fall asleep. I'm sure that's not out of boredom...or is it?

I've learned how to share my music without actually playing in person in front of an audience. I have acquired some good recording equipment and now have recorded and posted more than 30 songs online on YouTube. My channel is Windward319.

Above my guitar stand is a framed picture of Dad and Mom. Often as I'm playing, I look up and utter a silent "thank you" to these loving folks who opened up this essential pathway of my life.

I've tried to do the same thing for my own two sons, who now have at least four guitars I've given them. I hope they've meant as much to them as mine have to me.

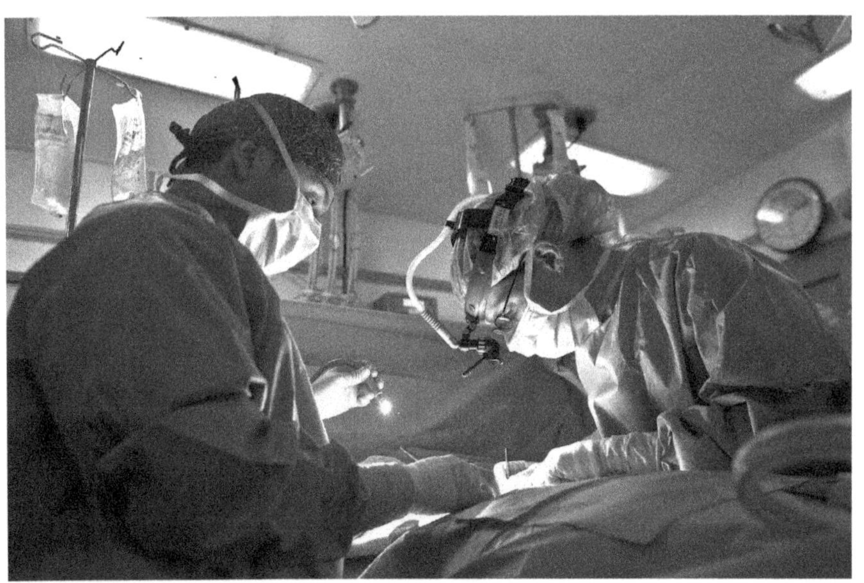

Surgeons doing what they do best. But is surgery always needed?
Pixabay

4

Mad Max, My Hernia, and Me

When I was in the sixth grade back in Oklahoma, my teacher Mr. Blackwell came to me one day and congratulated me on being named captain of the Kiwanis Junior Police for our school, Westside

Elementary. Growing up, few honors meant more to me than that one. Wow! I was now in charge of all the student crossing guards!

But then Mr. Blackwell saddened the moment unintentionally by saying, "You know, Jimmy, now that you are in a leadership position at school, you really should consider choosing your friends more wisely! You don't want to have students think you condone bad behavior by making friends of those who act badly. And I think you know who I am talking about."

Yes, I did know, and he was talking about my best friend, Max Hogan, a fellow sixth- grader. I never considered Max as "bad" before, although he was one of our class clowns who we jokingly dubbed *Mad Max*. He just liked to have fun and stretch the rules a bit. Nothing bad, though, at least not to me.

I had no intention of dumping Max as a friend, as Mr. Blackwell suggested, even though I knew my teacher felt he was looking out for my own good. And of course, I wasn't going to argue over it with the man who had a teacher's leverage on me. So, I responded dutifully to my teacher's concern:

"Oh sure. No trouble there! I'll be careful, Sir!"

Alas, the more I came to like being captain of the junior police, the more I feared losing the title. Continuing to hang out with Max could cause that if Mr. Blackwell were right. So, I began hanging out less and less with my friend. Our closeness suffered. We lost track of each other over time, and it hurt. I was not happy with myself.

What had not hurt before, hurt now. And, it was needless, because Mr. Blackwell was a really nice guy. He would have never caused me trouble if I had continued hanging out with Max.

All this came back to me just last week, some 68 years after the sixth grade. I was lying on my back in a hospital's post-op room, feeling the kind of pain the Physician's Desk Reference describes, nonsensically, as *"exquisite."*

I had just opted for umbilical hernia surgery after my doctor had warned me a few months back that I shouldn't wait for that *"trouble-*

maker" to break through the stomach wall and produce "ten-out-of-ten-level pain."

The surgery had just ended a half-hour ago, I was reentering the world I'm told is real, the general anesthesia was wearing off, and I was feeling every new stitch on my ripped-open gut.

"CRAP" was my first loud, post-op uttering, borne out of severe stomach pain. Whereupon I discovered instantly I was not alone in the recovery room.

A nurse's voice, struggling to remain calm, came slogging through the fog.

"Please turn to your left," Mr. Willis, "and look at our pain chart. "Then tell us where your pain level is."

On the wall were stick-drawn happy faces, solemn faces, and crying faces with the numbers 1-10 inked below them: the standard universal scale of agony, seemingly dumbed down for kindergarteners.

"I can't relate my pain to your chart!" I shouted. "Your scale only goes to 10!'

Unfazed, she repeated, "Where are you on our chart, Sir?"

"My pain's not on your stupid chart!" I reiterated. "It's *off* the damned chart!"

Then, for a reason that must have made sense to me, I continued, "I know what pain is. *I have a PhD!*"

Then it struck: I had just uttered a classic non sequitur that made me look like a world-class elitist or maybe just a fool. I looked around and saw what appeared to be a half-dozen faces all staring straight at me, quizzically.

I heard my interior voice go, *"Oops!"*

"Look, I'm *sorry!*" I said. "My pain is doing the talking. I'm sorry but ..."

"You're fine, Sir!" came another voice quickly. "It's all good!" chimed in another cheerily.

"Just let me apologize, okay?" I shouted. "I'm being a jerk!"

Another voice jumped in. "Should we bump him up another 5mg hydrocodone?"

"Can't," the surgeon said. "We've already maxed him out on pain meds."

Then a nurse asked me: "Sir, do you have a *low threshold* to pain?"

I paused. Compared to what? I thought. Being mauled by a grizzly bear? I didn't want to sound like the hospital wimp but, here again was another low-level concern.

"I don't know how to answer that question," I said. "The pain's as bad as a jagged *kidney stone,* if that helps. Crap, that's why I *had* this hernia surgery ... to *avoid* this level of pain. The hernia wasn't bothering me until now!"

The surgeon smiled. "The hernia was bigger than I expected."

And then someone in the ER decided to *grade* the operation, announcing, "And the surgery was excellent!"

Then the nurse who had, by this time, given up on me and the pain chart, gave me what was now a *command.*

"Mr. Willis, I need you to breathe! You *have to breathe!*"

Questions swirled inside me. *So now what? Was I not breathing? If not, how was I alive and talking? Had I crossed over? Is this heaven? Is heaven actually a torture chamber?*

All I could think of to say was, "I *am* breathing."

Then a sweet voice next to me said, "No Jim, You're not breathing deeply enough."

It was my wife Anne, and I started calming down for the first time.

"You have to take very *deep* breaths, Jim, so your lungs can fill and prevent pneumonia," she said. But it sounded like something an engineer might say when giving instructions on how to tighten bolts in a bridge span.

I appreciated her advice, but implementing it was a problem. I was not an iron bolt, but a guy who felt deep, stabbing pains every time I inhaled past a whisper.

Anne handed me a plastic suction device like a cop's breathalyzer. But instead of *blowing* into it, I was supposed to *inhale deeply* and watch the little colored ball rise to the level marked "deep breathing." I tried to suck on the tube and met this result:

My sucking sucked.

The ball failed to inch upwards at all. And each time it did move a bit, a knife stabbed my gut. I gave up after a few tries.

"Admit him!" the surgeon announced. "We can't send him home like this."

The post-op staff and drop-ins began leaving the room reluctantly, worried they'd miss my *next act,* and my own thoughts moved elsewhere. I began thinking of my sixth-grade pal, Max Hogan, and wondering what he might pull at a time like this, just for laughs. And then I wondered *why* I was even thinking about him at all? What connection did Mad Max have to any of this?

Instantly, the answer came.

Mr. Blackwell had warned me to remove Max from my life, just like this surgeon had warned me to remove my hernia from my stomach! Even though neither was causing me any pain until I bid them goodbye.

I wondered: If Max and I had made up, couldn't my *hernia* and I become close again, sometime down the road? I remembered another friend, Larry, telling me the other day he had lived with his hernia for many years and never had surgery for it.

So, was all this pain really needed? I mean, all close relationships are subject to risks, aren't they?

By now, though, I was headed for the hoped-for solitude of a private room upstairs and the promise of pain-free, opioid-induced sleep. What could go more wrong than this morning had? After all, Mom always told me, "Bad beginnings make for good endings, Son!"

The next morning, I was awakened at 5:30 by a 20-something blonde nurse who could have passed for a college cheerleader and who liked to call me *Buddy*.

"You're all stopped up! Gotta get you to pee, Buddy!" she said. "Looks like we're going to have to run an in-and-out catheter through you, Buddy!" she said with an exaggerated frown. But she was overly optimistic. It would take *three* different sized catheters and 20 minutes of a distinctly different kind of pain before she finished.

When she did, she smiled and said, "Sorry about the torture, Buddy! I think you have a swollen prostate. It's hard to get the catheter past that dude!"

I just lay there and looked up at the ceiling. When I looked down at my stomach, I saw I'd lost another friend, too. And this friendship dated back to the morning of my birth.

My belly button was gone.

I was shocked. No one told me *that* was going to happen. And out of the 25 or so authorizations I signed before surgery, essentially saying it would be okay if, by accident, the hospital killed me, I don't remember signing any doc that approved the removal of the last physical symbol of my birth connection to Mom. Yet there was the suture line that ran just like railroad tracks right through my umbilicus, decimating it.

I stared at my buttonless belly for a few minutes, wondering if tears would be appropriate.

"I'm sorry, Max," I sighed. I liked Mr. Blackwell, but I should not have listened to him about you."

5

Summer Memories

The ice cream man from days gone by.
Pixabay

I heard it again just yesterday,
    and it sounded just like it did 70 years ago.
This time it was on Buckingham Lane in Kentucky;
In 1955, it was on East Lockheed Drive in Oklahoma.
Its sound was faint at first, then slowly gained volume.

As it passed our house, it was at full decibel.
   It seemed the sound of a ... xylophone? No, a calliope.
From the circus of a bygone day.
Its tune could have come from an old movie cartoon,
   Tom and Jerry or Mighty Mouse, maybe.
It was full of lightness and memories of childhood fun
on a simmering, sunny, summer day.
   A memory reel replayed of a carefree growing-up afternoon,
playing football in the yard with friends,
where the nothing specialness of the day
was punctuated by the prospect of a cold, delicious treat.
   The sound was, of course, the ice cream truck,
announcing its arrival to every kid – and dog –
in the whole neighborhood.
   Its sound was greeted by loud cheers
and even-louder barking.
We paused our backyard play
to rush inside to ask Mom for a nickel
to exchange for a frozen Dreamsicle or Fudgesicle.
   Today, of course, we'd each need two dollars
to buy the same treat. Inflation bestows no respect
on childhood memories.
   Neither does fashion nor advances in transportation.
What used to be a smiling man in a five-pointed cap,
dressed in white long-sleeved shirt, and pants
with only a red bow tie and suspenders offering contrast,
was now a weary driver dressed in shorts, flip flops,
and stained t-shirt,
pedaling not a bicycle pushing a wheeled freezer ...
but driving a van contorted into a rolling snack shack,
holding up traffic as it snailed along at five miles per hour,
beckoning its young customers and yapping dogs.

Though I could still smell the old bicycle fridge,
emitting an unmistakable, memorable aroma
of good humor taste,
That smell was now gone,
replaced by carbon emission from the van.
    At least the soundtrack sounded the same.
Truth be told, though,
the ice cream tasted different too.
And, like the original Coca Cola
from the glass bottles of the 1950s,
Not nearly as good.

Oklahoma's proud Indian heritage is featured in its state flag.

6

We Were Not All Cowboys

If you grew up in the 1950s, especially in a state like Oklahoma, you probably spent at least a few years of your childhood playing Cowboys and Indians. And, especially in Oklahoma, your alter ego could have been either one, since that state was once officially named Indian Territory by the federal government.

We were proud of the history and the contributions both cowboys and Indians made to our state.

So, when *The Lone Ranger* anchored Saturday morning television, many of us paid just as much attention to Tonto as to the masked man.

Our state was known for its rich Indian heritage. During the 1830s, the U.S. government removed eastern Indian tribes to Indian Territory.

These people included the Cherokee, Creek, Seminole, Chickasaw, and Choctaw tribes. They came to be called the Five Civilized Tribes, because they prized education for their tribal members. It was a Cherokee tribesman, Sequoyah, who completed a Cherokee "syllabary" in 1821 that enabled that tribe to read and write. The Cherokees thus became one of the first North American tribes to gain a written language.

That, in turn, provided a means of unifying a people with new means of communication and a sense of independence.

As the next 25 years ensued, the Cherokee Nation had attained nearly a 100 percent rate of literacy. Turns out, that was higher than their white settler neighbors.

Other southeastern tribes that were "removed" to Oklahoma included the Alabama. Later, around the time of the Civil War and afterward, removed tribes from the Northeast would join them—the Delaware, Sac and Fox, Shawnee, Potawatomi, Kickapoo, Peoria, Ottawa, Wyandotte, Seneca, and Iowa. Prairie tribes included the Kaw, Ponca, Otoe, and Missouri.

The Indian Wars of the 1870s produced "reservations" in the Oklahoma region for Plains tribes such as the Comanche, Kiowa, Cheyenne, Arapaho, and others.

Geronimo, named of course for the famed Apache warrior who surrendered to the U.S. Army in 1988 and lived out his life as a farmer on an Apache reservation near Fort Sill. Before he died in 1909, he was invited by President Theodore Roosevelt to participate in TR's 1905 inauguration parade.

Native American pride is definitely a part of Oklahoma, and no kid would have objected to playing the role of Geronimo when the rifles, bows and arrows came out of the closet for some backyard playtime.

For me and other young Sooners, playing with those rubber-suction arrows later morphed into participating in the sport of archery, and many top archers came from our state. I still remember achieving my Archery merit badge as a Boy Scout in my hometown of Midwest City, and I stayed with the sport on into my30s.

To be sure, relationships with white European settlers in the state were not always easy. Life was harsh, and it was sometimes bloody, as books and films like the 2023 book and film, *Killers of the Flower Moon* depicted. Even when some tribes became rich because of oil finds on their land, tragedy often accompanied their success as ruthless companies and families stole those mineral rights and -- in some cases -- the land itself.

As the Oklahoma Historical Society notes on its website, "American Indians living in Oklahoma have a complicated, interesting and unique history. Their story involves hardship, tribal and individual victories, clashes of cultures, and juxtaposed realities with the American mainstream."

It took time for Oklahoma settlers to understand and appreciate the fact that these Indians operated on different values than most non-Indians. To the Native American, elemental forces of creation—the sun, water, earth, and wind—guided their daily lives. Daily rituals of life and many traditional ceremonies continued to be practiced on a regular basis and continued to evolve as the Indigenous cultures reemerged and readapted to new conditions, the Historical Society notes.

The oral tradition of storytelling preserved legends about important leaders and events and also recorded verbal accounts of new experiences and leaders. Thus, tribal accounts of the past continue to be based on oral tradition, rather than written, documentary sources.

"The survival and success of Oklahoma Indians incorporates several significant themes. One theme involves a learned, shared experience that comprises a presumptive 'collective identity' called Oklahoma Indian."

These Native Americans brought their collective experience of triumph and tragedy, defeat, and survival to Oklahoma when they were sent here by the federal government. They were accustomed to losing and then rebuilding their homes and their realities. They became experts in adapting to new realities while still holding on to their own native traditions.

Part of that tradition was found in the tribal dances that they still perform and celebrate in Oklahoma.

When I was a freshman at the University of Oklahoma, one of my dorm mates was a full-blooded Cherokee who performed these dances in many state celebrations of his and other tribes. I still remember him donning his full tribal regalia one late night and inadvertently scaring the daylights out of my roommate, who was *not* an Indian. Knowing his sense of humor, though, I was never sure that was an accident!

Native logic is based on the belief that both physical and metaphysical forces help shape daily life. The tribes of Oklahoma also see life from a *communal* viewpoint, and they also tend to think in circular fashion. Day changing into night is one such cycle, as is the full moon's monthly repetition, and the changing of the seasons which complete a cycle every year.

A clear indication of how important Indian tribes were to Oklahoma is found in the names of many of the state's towns and counties are: Choctaw, Chickasaw, Kiowa, Seminole, Cherokee, Potawatomi, Shawnee, Pawnee, Ponca City, Tonkawa, Tahlequah, and the list goes on.

Native logic is based on the belief that both physical and metaphysical forces help shape daily life. The tribes of Oklahoma also see life from a communal viewpoint, and they also tend to think in circular fashion. Day changing into night is one such cycle, as is the full moon's monthly repetition, and the changing of the seasons which complete a cycle every year.

So, the concept of "the circle of life" is an important one to Native Americans. The stories they tell and the dances they perform make the past come alive. In like manner, their prophecies "bring the future back to the present in a time continuum. This is Indian reality; this is the thought pattern of Oklahoma traditional Indians," write the Oklahoman historians.

As youngsters growing up in Oklahoma, most of us were unaware of all this, however. That was grown-up talk, and history was a class in school. All we knew is that our Indian friends -- who we probably didn't even know *were* Indians -- were simply our friends. They lived on our block, and we went to school with them.

Some might have looked a bit different, but what did we care? What mattered was we liked them, they liked us, and most seemed good at every sport from tetherball to baseball.

And I'm sure there were times in our backyard games when they themselves played the cowboy, while we played the Indian.

7

Hayley Mills, Me, and the Skytrain Theater

Falling in Love at the Skytrain Theater
Pixabay

I've spent a lot of time writing about growing up in the then-new Oklahoma town of Midwest City after my family moved there in 1949 when I was only 3. My guiding question in those reflections has been, *how much of who I am today is where I'm from?*

I've realized one challenge that keeps more writers from crafting a book about their hometown experiences is the question of just how much they can actually remember from those young years? And then there are those things that you *do* remember, some of which were so foolishly dangerous that you wonder how you survived those times at all.

I've learned that at least four things help open more closed-door memories than I thought possible when I began this book: First, writing about one event often triggers a dormant memory about another. Second, going back to my hometown and seeing where I grew up and the places that made up my world help tremendously. Third, talking with childhood friends, most of whom I have not seen since school days, brings other memories back to life. And fourth, remembering *feelings* instead of trying to remember *events,* often leads me to those incidents and/or people who inspired those emotions.

Take, for example, the last of these triggers. *Can you remember when you first thought you fell in love and why?* For me, I was 13 years old and in the 7th grade when I walked two blocks to the Skytrain Theater one Saturday afternoon to see the 1959 Disney movie, *Parent Trap.*

It was hard enough for me to keep my eyes off its 13-year-old unknown British starlet, Hayley Mills, but the fact there were *two* of her in the film made it doubly hard. If you know the plot, you know she played identical twins named Sharon McKendrick and Susan Evers. The sisters' parents were divorced, and the two mischievous sisters devised a plan to reunite them. I must have used up two weeks' allowances going back to see the movie several times, each time falling deeper in love with that blonde, smiling Hayley Mills with the cutest upturned nose imaginable.

The featured song that the twins sang in the film instantly soared to No. 1 on my personal best song of the year. It was called, *Let's Get Together,* and I thought, "Sounds right to me!" And, being an aspiring writer myself and in love with the singers, I thought the lyrics reached the heights of great English literature. Especially all the *"yeah, yeah, yeahs!"*

To be honest, though, I should mention I'm still awaiting being awarded my *own* first Nobel Prize for Literature, as if my review of *Let's Get Together* doesn't suggest why.

Returning to the influence my town had on me, I would say this: If Bill Atkinson, had not included a movie theater in his plan for the Midwest City's *Original Mile,* there would have been no *Skytrain Theater.* That movie house was a prime example of how Atkinson was thinking about servicing the entertainment needs of children and teens, as well as their parents when he began building the town.

The Skytrain was named for the thousands of C-47 military transport planes built across the street at Tinker AFB. It opened its doors in November 1944 and was an instant hit with the kids. The theater was built for $95,000 and featured first-run films, a modern sound system, air conditioning, padded seats and paved parking. It showed five different movies each week, and Saturday morning matinees were designed for young children.

If I had not lived there, where the Skytrain was in walking distance from everyone's front door, I might *never* have seen that film at all, or at least not until I was older. If so, Hayley Mills would probably *not* have been my original love and, somehow, that doesn't seem right.

But I did grow up there, I did see the film, and I did fall in love with this young British starlet. A couple years later, when I started dating hometown girls, I remember being disappointed that they didn't look or sound like Hayley Mills. Until, that is, I met a blonde band majorette in my sophomore year of high school named Margaret Palmer. *Maggie* was a baton twirler, and her uniform was tight, white, and slight. If you've ever seen pictures of twirlers from the 60s, you know they were the first of the schoolgirls who had permission to wear miniskirts. And the white parade boots only added to the picture. To say the majorettes were popular with the guys would be an understatement.

More importantly, though, I felt Maggie could have been Hayley Mills' *second* sister, they looked so much alike. While she wasn't British so didn't have Hayley's accent, she did speak with what I found to be a happy voice, spiced at times with a charming lisp when she got excited. Maggie proved to be a great substitute for Hayley in the times we dated, since the gods of fate seemed to dictate I would never meet my secret love. Hollywood was a long way away.

As it turned out, Maggie and I became lifelong friends, although we lost track of each other for some 40 years before our paths crossed again in our senior years via high school reunions.

A postscript to Hayley and me, however, is that in the year 2008, I was living in Southern California and realized I had yet to bump into any movie stars. Then one day I was standing in the checkout line at a Chico's store in Manhattan Beach when I turned and noticed the woman right behind me. It was Hayley Mills.

She smiled at me and, before I could engage my mental filters and say something like, "It's a nice day, isn't it?" I let fly with, *"You don't know this, but I fell in love with you when I was 13."* Her smile broadened and said how sweet I was to say that, and we went our separate ways out into the Southern California sunshine. But my warm feeling inside came not from the sun but from finally meeting my first teenage love.

Although *The Parent Trap* was about the two young Hayleys ensnaring their onscreen parents, Miss Mills had unknowingly lured me into a different kind of trap. I'll never forget how good it felt when it snapped shut.

But here's the irony: In all my decades of dating, courtship, and marriage, up to the year 2000, there were only two blondes. The other 95 percent of the girls and women were not. And the one I've been lovingly married to for almost 26 years is the one I would *not* trade for Hayley Mills. Annie is a very striking *brunette* with the cutest *Kentucky* accent.

*(In part, expanded from material in my 2024 book, **Tinkertown**.)*

Kids' bikes can take them to new adventures, even as they remain in the city limits.
Pixabay

8

First Wheels of Freedom

When I think of my first bicycle, which my parents gave me at the age of 9, I think of two concepts: *freedom and balance*. Freedom because my bike automatically enlarged my world and my ability to travel it; balance because you can't ride one without learning it.

Although we kids did a lot more walking in the 50s than kids do today — my weekdays started with the five-block walk to elementary school. A bike meant we could get there faster and take a long, circuitous route home if we wished. And on weekends, we fantasized our bike could take us to the moon if we wanted.

To my memory, my bike was my first taste of freedom.

My red rocket

That first bike was a sleek red Schwinn, pretty much the Cadillac of bikes at the time. I called it my Red Rocket. It came from the only bike shop in town, owned by Gary Wiedeman's dad around the block. That fact that Gary's dad's world was bicycles automatically made Gary one of the most popular guys in the neighborhood.

As for balance, that was the challenge I faced in learning how to ride it. I still have a vivid memory of Dad taking me out on the driveway on Christmas Day and coaching me on how to keep my body from becoming one with the pavement. Of course, I only half-listened, eager to give it a try, and of course I took a couple spills.

I quickly found that if I just stopped *thinking* about how to balance and instead let my body become one with the bike on its own, it worked better. I was riding up and down the driveway by Christmas night.

A lifelong lesson

From that, I learned that I can't just think things into happening. I have to trust my body's ability to apply what I've learned. Throughout my life, I have found that to be a useful lesson, applied to many obstacles that need clearing from learning to play the piano and guitar, to swimming, platform diving, and SCUBA diving. Given a chance, our bodies can get along fine at times on nothing but an innate instinct and muscle memory.

When I let my mind direct difficult physical functions for my body, I've learned that my thoughts sometimes focus more on the fear factor: fear of falling, fear of failing, fear of looking foolish. So, overcoming the physical challenge is made even harder by overcoming our mind's flashing warning sign of fear.

For me, I've found it better to follow the Nike slogan: *Just Do It.*

From bikes to life

Finding balance is a lifelong process, and I long ago learned that balancing on a bike is far easier than keeping our lives on an even keel. The same principles of learning to ride my bike often apply to this greater adult challenge, however.

So today I was out in the garage, looking up at my Trek 7100 bike, hanging from the ceiling, and I realized I haven't been on it in well over a year. In fact, it serves another purpose now, as a hook to hang power cords on and as a collector of flying fur from our three dogs.

That saddened me, because that bike — like my first one — deserves a better fate. It has served me well, and I vowed to get it down, clean it off, hang the cords somewhere else, and take it out for a spin.

This patient teacher of balance and facilitator of freedom deserves that. And maybe I can recapture at least a bit of the wonder I felt as a boy with my shiny red Schwinn.

PS: Two days later, I took my trek down, cleaned it up and aired up the tires. Then I proudly mounted it and headed toward the end of the driveway. I never made it. My balance shifted, I reached for the ground to prop myself up, but I'd raised the seat so high, my foot didn't reach the pavement. My bike came crashing over, taking me hard into the pavement against my torn-miniscus knee.

Maybe I'll try again in a year or two.

9

Whatever Happened to Kid TV?

Foreman Scotty (Steve Powell) and the birthday kids of the "Circle 4 Ranch," sitting atop Woody.

WKY-TV Oklahoma City

I was 11 years old in 1957, my friends and I all had television sets, and some of our afternoon outdoor activities moved indoors.

It was the era that journalist and commentator Linda Ellerbee would write about later in her classic essay, **When Television Ate my Best Friend.** In that story, after a 6-year-old Linda mysteriously loses the outdoor companionship of her friend Lucy to this new thing called a "TV", she laments to her mother that television must *eat* people.

Her mother tells her not to worry, that television is only entertainment, and that she is getting one, too. Ellerbee writes, "Christmas arrived, and Santa Claus brought us a television. 'See?' my parents said. 'Television doesn't eat people.' Maybe not. But television changes people. It changed my family forever."

Outdoors comes indoors

Admittedly, the late 1950s was a watershed period when outdoor group activities turned more toward indoor activity, and that activity was watching TV, often alone although sometimes with your friends. Either way, we kids were all treated every afternoon to a local cowboy show for kids, produced in Oklahoma City at my dad's TV station, WKY, Channel 4. It was the *Foreman Scotty Show*, with a longer title of **Foreman Scotty and the Circle 4 Ranch** (just to give the station itself a daily plug). It was produced right in the studio and on its spacious back lot.

Merchandising the West

Every afternoon Foreman Scotty became embroiled in adventures, chasing the bad guys around makeshift sets that looked very real to youngsters who wanted them to be. In between the scripted adventures, Scotty would be back on the established set for the show, made to look like the inside of a barn, with 25 live, invited kids who were perched on benches or hay bales. On at least one occasion, I was one of those kids who sat in awe of my afternoon hero. The whole thing was a must-see for those of us in and around Midwest City and solidified our wish list for Christmas. We wanted anything from cap pistols and holsters, to cowboy hats or wooden horses that reminded us of Foreman Scotty and his Circle 4 Ranch.

Said one of our friends who looked back on the show years later, "If you grew up here and you're over 35, you know about Foreman Scotty. If you were a youngster then, you possibly were on the show."

The show ran for 14 years, and Scotty was played by a Tulsa acting student and WKY announcer Steve Powell, who died in 1994.

The Magic Lasso

As Ann DeFrange would write about his passing, "With other live television pioneers, he created characters who live in the cultural literacy of Local viewers. He created the corral where guests sat for the show; Woody the wooden horse where little birthday celebrants got to sit in honor on the uncomfortable saddle instead of the uncomfortable benches; the "Magic Lasso," which appeared on the screen to select the lucky kid who won the Golden Horseshoe; and the secret Password, *Nicksobilly.*"

Space cowboys

Danny Williams as 3-D Danny.

Not to be forgotten in the kids programming at WKY, however, was the 1950s interest in outer space. So, along with Foreman Scotty, WKY tapped one of its rising celebrities, Danny Williams, to become the futuristic spaceman, *Dan D. Dynamo, or just 3-D Danny.*

The latter name was a stroke of marketing genius, tying in as well to audience interest in the gimmicky new 3-dimensional-view movie exhibition fad. So, every afternoon, 3-D Danny would be furiously turning knobs on a control panel in the "Space Science Center" and, along with his trusted robot Bazark, would try desperately to save the world from aliens.

It even got to the point where 3-D Danny's futuristic world intersected with the western world of Foreman Scotty as some of the skits featured both heroes and Bazark masterfully chasing and subduing the bad guys around the Channel 4 backlot.

The Golden Age

The 1950s was the golden age of locally and regionally produced afternoon kids shows, and WKY-TV (which went on the air in 1949 and hired my dad that same year) was a true pioneer of this genre. It was part of the Oklahoma Publishing Company, owned by its founder E.K. Gaylord. He started the state's main daily newspaper, *The Daily Oklahoman*, and I would later work for it as a journalist.

In later years, Gaylord and Co. would produce the nationally syndicated *Buck Owens Show* and *Hee Haw* from the same WKY studio, then the family would go on to take over Opryland in Nashville and build the Opryland Hotel.

A hero on my block

As a child on Lockheed Drive, I became something of a neighborhood celebrity because Dad worked at WKY, and he often would invite me and my sister C.J., along with a few of our friends, to come watch some of the live shows from the observation booth above the studio. One of our favorite shows was the Saturday Night Wrestling program, where they set up a ring right on the studio floor, surrounded by chairs for the live audience, and brought in professional wrestlers to grind it out.

(This chapter was adapted from my 2024 book, *Tinkertown: A Wheatfield, an Airbase, and Us)*

10

Memories of my Dad

W.J. Willis, my dad.

All week long I've been thinking about my dad. I think it was coming across my old camera that triggered the memory. That story will unfold below. For whatever reason, in the end, a lifetime of memories must somehow be boiled down to a few indelibly defining images for easy recall.

But why *these* images?

I don't have the answer to that; just the images. And they involve a Dairy Queen, a diner, and a darkroom. I think they may stand out because they show the importance of a caring act, a dream, and a kind of grand design.

A banana splat

It was a hot summer afternoon in Oklahoma, and my dad had taken me over to the local Dairy Queen for a cold treat. We were standing at one of two walk-up windows and I was watching as they made my chocolate dip cone and wondering two things: why didn't the ice cream tumble into the jug of hot sauce when it went in Q-first, and how did they get that sauce to harden so fast?

Science was never my strong suit, though, so I decided to focus on enjoying the treat.

As Dad and I stepped from the window, a young boy at the next window had just stepped back, tripped and smashed his fully-loaded banana split into the hot pavement. His tears came instantly as he saw what was probably his week's allowance dissolve before him in the summer sun.

He was alone, and my dad helped him to his feet, patted him, and dusted him off. Then, without hesitation, Dad turned back to the window and ordered this youngster a brand-new dessert treat.

I will never outlive this memory of a man, who I always felt was so emotionally reserved, being moved to spend an extra buck he probably needed, to buy an unknown kid a new banana split.

In an instant, I knew why I loved and trusted Dad so much.

A joint called John's

Saturdays brought eating lunch out with Dad, often after a trip to Sears to inspect the new power saws. Could it be Dad and I were bonding over food?

Regardless, the fact was we didn't have many eateries in my hometown during the 1950s and early 1960s, but we did have one favorite spot. You could call it a diner, but only because it *looked* like one. You'd be more accurate in calling it a burger joint, and I only ever knew it as *John's* cause that's what Dad always called it.

My mom and sister might accompany us maybe one other night a week there, but this Saturday lunch date would usually belong to just Dad and me. The hamburgers were pretty good, but it was more fun just watching Dad eat up the atmosphere.

We would go in, stake out a couple stools close to where the eponymous owner would be flipping burgers on the grill, and he and Dad would start in talking.

They would go on about everything from Sooner football to the new burger place called McDonald's opening up in Oklahoma City. Neither thought the place would succeed by selling hamburgers for 15 cents each when everyone else was selling them for twice that.

A ticket to ride

It wasn't long before I realized Dad was letting me ride along on his dream of owning his *own* burger place one day and shed his angst-ridden advertising job in the process. On many nights he would come home, plop down in his easy chair and thumb through his dining services or restaurant supply trade magazines, looking for ideas on how to design his own diner one day.

He and John would talk about it as the burgers fried on the grill.

"Jim, the real key is to get customers in and out fast," John would say. "Why do you think I have those bar stools at the counter instead of tables and chairs? Nobody wants to sit around all day on a bar stool chatting. Once they're done eating, they get up and leave."

Made sense to Dad, although, he would regularly disprove John's logic, as their conversation would go on well after our plates were clean.

But I came to realize how important Dad's dream was when he was feeling trapped in a day that was going nowhere. I learned what an escape valve those dreams can provide. My father never followed through on his vision, mostly because of the duty he felt toward providing for his family. But that never made the dream itself unimportant.

Magic from a dark place

Dad also found solace in his hobbies, and art was a big one. He was visually talented and he moved seamlessly from sketching, to photography, to oils and pastels. In my youngest years I learned sketching from him, but it was his instruction in photography that got my attention. And that kept it for life.

I was in my early teens when Dad showed me how to take pictures, develop film, print and enlarge pictures in a darkroom he built in our garage. I was fascinated by the magic that came from that place and from simple black-and-white photography.

From about age 14 forward, my Christmas wish list featured an endless list of cameras, film, chemicals, photo paper, enlargers, timers, print dryers, and so on. I would shoot pictures of everything I saw and figured out how to make money by transferring photos of new homes onto post card stock and then selling those post cards to the buyers of the new real estate.

It becomes a calling

When I began shooting pictures for my high school newspaper, *The Bomber Beam,* my journalism career was officially launched. I would transition into writing but wound up using photography to help illustrate my stories.

On my most important series of stories, covering the aftermath of the Oklahoma City bombing in 1995, I used my telephoto lens to focus in on small vignettes I would not have seen without the camera.

I remember one moving memorial service, right on the rubble, just before the implosion of the building's carcass two weeks after the bombing. There were the sad expressions of the three hard-hat workers who stared in disbelief at the bombed-out Federal Building from the remains of a neighboring building; there was the bright red rose jutting out of the Reuters photographer's tripod, and there was the heavily scuffed and bent orange highway cone, kicked by one too many angry first-responders who had just found another body part of a victim.

All these went into my stories and were the focus of my photos.

Together, these words and pictures would cause me to receive the kind of compliment any journalist prizes highly: *You made me feel like I was there.* And when I heard that, I thought, maybe. *But it was* my *dad who showed me how to make you feel like you were there.*

Reversing the image

As I've reflected on my dad's influence in my life, it's hard to imagine there were times when I discounted that influence. There was a time when I felt he and I didn't have that much in common, and that we never bonded the way I thought other fathers and sons were doing.

I was wrong. Dad and I were more alike than I allowed myself to realize and our bonding didn't come over deep, long conversations, but simply by spending time together in situations like those described above.

In some ways it was like the reverse image that reveals itself when the negative image on film morphs into the positive image on the paper to which it is projected. It takes a shot of light and some chemistry to make that happen.

And those are exactly the same two things that made it happen for my dad and me.

It took awhile to get used to swimming without the Speedos.
Pixabay

11

Scouting in the Buff

I grew up in an Air Force town in Oklahoma, a town that sprang up out of wheat fields in 1942 as a place to house the military and civilian workforce at Tinker AFB.

My family moved there in 1949, and it seemed to me that the names of all the men were preceded by a "Sergeant," "Lieutenant," or

"Colonel." Every street in town had a name related to airplanes or hero pilots.

That's where our Lockheed Drive came from, just one street over from Boeing, and a stone's throw from General Senter Avenue.

Scouting just fit

So my town was a patriotic one, and the military, church, and a set of conservative rules and values permeated it all. Hence, scouting seemed a natural fit, and there were a lot of green and khaki uniforms to be seen.

Tuesday night was Boy Scout night from about 5th grade through 7th for me. It was about the only socially structured event on my weekly schedule, except for church on Sunday mornings. Both events took place in the Wickline Methodist Church just around the block from our home.

Like all the other scouts, I began as a Tenderfoot, worked my way through the Second and First Class ranks, and then earned enough merit badges to become a Star Scout.

I was two ranks away from the top, but my growing sense of independence and interest in girls pulled me away from scouting for a couple years, and I never made Eagle.

I did return to it as a sophomore, however, when I joined the post-graduate group of scouts known as Explorers. My fondest memories were of those three years. There was less structure and more exploring of your possible career interests in life.

All in all, I think Scouting helped me in the initial stages of growing up. As I mentioned to a friend recently, earning merit badges like Home Repairs came in handy when I had to replace two windows I broke by hitting baseballs through them.

I also learned about gun safety, camping, public service, and a host of other things, including what poison ivy looks (and feels) like. In Scouting, the more merit badges you accumulate, the more you learn. It's sound theory, assuming you do the work yourself and don't farm it out to your dad while you sit back and watch.

I also honed some aquatic skills that served as the springboard for getting lifeguard certification which got me several years worth of lifeguard jobs that saw me through college. Those jobs also got me a lot of summertime dates.

All this said, there was this one quirky — if not totally bizarre — memory from my Scouting years that I still have trouble believing, even though I lived it many times as a teenager. Maybe I should just spit it out instead of trying to finesse it:

Both as a Boy Scout and an Explorer, we would go swimming at the YMCA in Oklahoma City, and the Y had this strange rule that our swimming had to be done in the buff. Turns out, a whole bunch of high schools around the country had the same rule.

Yup. We all swam *nude*.

It wasn't mixed gender swimming, but it still felt weird. Feels even weirder as it pops into memory today.

Every time I talk about this — and believe me, I don't do it much because it sends younger family members screaming into the night — I still find myself asking internally: "Did this really happen, or is this some crazy dream that's haunting me?"

Having a bunch of boys and their adult leaders swimming naked takes on a more ominous cast when you think about all the recent lawsuits over perversion in the ranks of scoutmasters over the decades.

I strongly suspect many Baby Boomers have the same unsettling memory. Here's one that comes from a guy in New York City who was having lunch with a friend in Manhattan when her dad began talking about his own memory of nude swimming at the Y. He writes:

"Nude-nude?" I asked. "Totally nude," he said.

He remembers the instructor telling them something about it being more sanitary that way. "But," he conceded, "no one really questioned it." After a moment, he paused.

"What the hell was that all about?"

Checking some American history, I discovered that nude swimming wasn't a Boy Scout mandate, but a YMCA practice, as well as the norm at thousands of American high schools. It followed a mandate from the American Public Health Association from 1926 until 1962. The feeling was that skinny dipping was more hygienic and sanitary than using a suit. Some Y's kept the practice going another 10 years beyond that.

If you're one of the lucky ones who missed out on all this and still needs more proof that all this isn't an early April Fools joke, check out this YouTube video called, "Nude Swimming in School."

These memories don't wash off.

As I look back on my scouting years, there were two non-erase memories amid those others that fade into a collective blur.

The first is of my very first overnight camping trip as an 11-year-old Tenderfoot and the extreme case of homesickness I suffered through that night, even though Mom, Dad, my dog Laddie, and home were only 20 minutes away.

And the second was letting it all fly from the high dive at the Y with some 30 other nude guys swimming around in the crystal clear water down below.

Think I'll shove that one back into the locker for another decade or so.

12

At Dawn, We Attack!

Fighter planes and writers often like to attack the enemy at dawn.
Pixabay

For this career writer, the blank page has always been the enemy. It must be attacked and subdued, and it's best to do that as the enemy still slumbers.

That's how a lot of my writing has survived on the battlefield of crowded days.

Case in point: one night in 1990 as I lay dreaming. I've always been a dreamer, so it wasn't surprising when an inaudible voice appeared that night uttering the enigmatic phrase, *The Shadow World.*

Excuse me?

I had no idea what it meant, although as a journalist, I figured it had something to do with the world I was presenting through my reporting and writing.

I rolled over and wrote that phrase down, knowing if I didn't, I would forget it by morning.

Dawn came early that day, but I was up before the sun. I climbed out of bed and went immediately to my desktop computer to start expanding on my dream phrase.

A book is born

Before I knew it, a few hours had passed and I was 25 pages into creating what would become my third published book: *The Shadow World: Life Between the News Media and Reality.*

The publisher's description shows what I came up with: *"This book looks at the news media's portrayal of reality and seeks answers as to why this portrayal often falls short of reality itself. Jim Willis examines the factors that contribute to the journalist's often faulty perception of reality, factors that are beyond the immediate control of the reporter: errant sources, competitive influences, the embedding process of storytelling, marketing's influence on the news, and the structure of news stories."*

The dream meets the dawn

So now you know what a fun guy I must be to be entertaining such adventurous and romantic dreams as that. But the fact that this untethered thought became a *book* is more credited to the effect that *dawn* has on a writer's creative juices.

The dream may have given me the subject, but the early dawn hours gave me the verb. Along with those verbs came, as the late commentator Paul Harvey used to say, *"the rest of the story."*

I've always loved the early pre-dawn hours, feeling that my mind was at its clearest, my filters were at a low point, and so were the mental distractions that the rest of the day always brings. When I am jumping into an idea, like *The Shadow World*, I don't need distractions and I don't need filters. The latter are very useful when it comes later in the editing process, but not in the initial draft of my work. This is a time to just let it all flow and, for me, the hours of 4:30 to 7:30 a.m. have often been those best hours.

But why?

I've done a little research to discover if that holds true for other writers, and I've found it does for many of them. Here are two reasons cited by fellow writer Naomi Pham:

1. *Early morning is the time when you're most energetic.* Working in the first hours of the day can, therefore, improve your productivity and performance. You'll have a better creativity flow, greater focus, and re-silience, which translates into much faster-writing speed.

2. *Your willpower is at its highest.* Social psychologist Roy Baumeister once conducted an experiment testing willpower. Two groups of people were led into a room filled with the aroma of freshly-baked cookies. The table before them held a plate of cookies and a plate of radishes.

One group was asked to taste the cookies, and the other, the radishes. Then both groups were given a complex geometric puzzle to solve. The cookies were left on the table with no instructions not to eat them. Those who ate the radishes and resisted the cookie temptation gave up within 8 minutes, while the cookie-eaters hung on for 19.

The conclusion

Baumeister concluded that our willpower is a *limited source*. It runs out as we make use of it. The longer that day goes on, the more we have to use our willpower. So it is strongest in the early-morning hours. As the day progresses, we're more likely to put off writing out of laziness and mental exhaustion.

Then comes age

Now at 77, I dream about getting up early to attack my writing, but the flesh has become weaker than the spirit. it's just harder than it used to be to get out of bed early. So I start writing a little later, then a little later than that, then — some days — it's time for bed again.

Still, it doesn't mean my writing doesn't get done. Just takes a little longer, as do most things as we age. Happily, there is more free time in retirement than when I was writing and teaching for a living.

Work expands to the time

So, I've spent the past 14 months writing my memoirs. At 400 pages it's one of the longer books I've done, but it's also taken about 400 days and nights to finish it. There was a time I would have knocked it out in half that time.

It's just that, these nights, my battle-hardened troops need all the sleep they can get before attacking that dreaded blank page once again.

A replica of my "Black Bear" Firebird TransAm Turbo in 1978.

13

My Year as a Bandit

I suppose the overarching question for the following story would be, *"At what age does maturity kick in for a guy?"* It seems to fit what some folks were thinking about me at the time.

If I were to name a time when some of my self-image fantasies came true (at least for a while), it would be 1978. I was living in Dallas, finishing up a decade as a newspaper editor, and about to move to Missouri to start work on a Ph.D. in Journalism at the University of Missouri, where I would also become a member of the faculty.

Sounds very grown-up, right? Not quite. That dream of college teaching was all falling into place nicely, but my *really* cool fantasy materialized when I decided to become the Burt Reynolds character of Bandit from the newly released film, *Smokey and the Bandit.*

Of course, to do that, I had to acquire a new Pontiac *Firebird TransAm Turbo* (subtly identified on the road by the giant flaming, gold firebird image splayed all across the hood of this black beast.)

My life was about to get interesting.

I was 32 at the time when my ubiquitous impulsiveness drove me to the dealership where I parted company with my reliable, but too middle-aged Ford Galaxy. I swapped it out for my very own Bandit car. I already had the cowboy hat and boots, so I was ready to go rule the streets of Dallas.

Maybe I should put my reasoning (let's call it that, anyway) into context first. Two years earlier, I felt a seismic shift take place in my brain. For me, the 30th birthday was a hard one to swallow. A milestone. I felt I was leaving youthfulness behind and was entering the "establishment." That was not a good thought for Baby Boomers like me who had just come out of the rebellious 1960s and early 70s where the most popular mantra among us was *"Never trust anyone over 30."*

My uneasiness was fueled by a movie that had recently premiered called *Logan's Run.* It was sci-fi, and its premise was the world had become overcrowded by the 23rd century, so everyone who reached their 30th birthday was exterminated to make room for the younger, more vigorous population.

So, my reaction to all this was to go buy the car of a young man's fantasy. No need to advertise I was heading toward middle-age, or so I thought.

A couple hours after buying the TransAm, I was out on Lemon Avenue showing off my new wheels to anyone who cared to stop and drop their jaw. I pulled my newly-named "Black Bear" up to a stoplight near Love Field. Up next to me pulls a Dodge Charger with a teen behind the wheel. He looked my way, smiles, and yells to me, "Wanna race?"

"Why not?" the idiot behind my wheel yelled back.

The revving of engines began, each of us trying to out-growl the other, and then the light flashed green. Tires spun as our two rockets launched into what was mercifully an empty street ahead. It was road bliss for the thirty seconds it lasted as I left the Firebird wannabe in the smoke of my turbo's exhaust.

Oh, and did I forget to mention my then-wife was sitting in the passenger seat while all this was occurring? If so, chalk it up to my PTSD, because she was in a fighting mood, only not with the guys in the Charger, and I was outgunned.

"Holy CRAP, Jim!" she bellowed. "How *old* did you say you were? Is our marriage even legal, or did I rob the crib? NEVER do that again when – if ever again -- I'm in this smokewagon!"

Although my self-image was shrinking rapidly under this (well-deserved) verbal assault, I did like the term she used to describe my Black Bear, and I considered changing its name to *Smokewagon*. But, given her mood, vis-à-vis me and my car, I decided not to use her name for it after all.

A couple days later, my wife was back to normal, although still refusing to get into my new car again.

That's when I decided to add one other feature to my fantasy machine. I bought a CB radio and had it installed under the dash. If you remember the 70s, well over half the male population (and a good percentage of females) were chatting it up on the highways with CBs.

Within a week or two, I had mastered the vocabulary and protocol of my fellow road warriors (most of whom were truckers), and my new favorite film was the Kris Kirsofferson/Ali McGraw action flick, *Convoy*. You can't make a rogue trucker film without featuring CB-speak, and this film had plenty of it.

"C'mon, C'mon Good Buddy! This is the Black Bear out here on the flip side of 66, trying to say a few klicks ahead of Smokey. Ten-four, come back?"

It was fun while it lasted, but it didn't last long. A few months later I had to sell the Bear to help pay the lawyer for the divorce when my wife came to her senses in Missouri and decided my level of maturity was just a tick lower than she needed (or deserved, I might add). So, I bought a second-hand AMC Javelin AMX which, while definitely flexing its biceps over the front wheels, finished a distant second to my TransAm. It was a smaller fantasy, yet it was one I could afford.

But I did keep my CB radio.

Hello, Reality. Goodbye, Bandit.

The City Meat Market became the Sandhill Curiosity Shop in Erick, Oklahoma.

14

A Town Called Erick

What is it about small towns, anyway? Especially towns in your own home state that you've never had any connection with, and yet somehow you connect to them instantly the first time you enter them.

Maybe it was the circumstance that brought me here, or the mood I was in, but the tiny Western Oklahoma town of Erick fit that bill for me.

First off, I am from Oklahoma, so I have a special interest in its towns. But Erick was such a departure from where I was living this time in 2014, I couldn't help but feel I'd wandered into a 1960s episode of *The Twilight Zone.* You know, one of the several plot lines where a motorist leaves the highway to get gas and finds himself in another world entirely, probably 50 years earlier.

A post office, originally named Dennis, was established to serve the local community on November 8, 1900. This community developed along the Choctaw, Oklahoma and Gulf Railroad line (later the Chicago, Rock Island and Pacific Railway), built in 1902. On November 16, 1901, the name was changed to honor Beeks Erick, the townsite developer and president of the Choctaw Townsite and Improvement Company, and the town incorporated that year.

I was living in Los Angeles in 2014 and making one of my long road trips home to Oklahoma to see my folks when I drove into Erick a dozen years ago. It wasn't totally a serendipitous stop, however, because I'd heard of this town before and been curious about it. It's just located so far out in the plains that I seldom passed by it.

I had heard of Erick because of two celebrities that grew up there and found fame in Hollywood. One was the singer Roger Miller ("King of the Road," "Dang Me," "You Can't Roller Skate in a Buffalo Herd") and the other was the lesser-known Sheb Wooley. Honest to Pete, that was his character's name he played on the 1960s TV western series, Rawhide. Pete was a trailhand with Gil Favor's cattle drive every Friday night on this acclaimed series that also gave an unknown Clint Eastwood his start as Rowdy Yates.

Miller was at the top of the pop and country charts back then. But his was an unlikely beginning to a success story. He was born in Fort Worth, but his poverty-stricken parents sent him to grow up with relatives on a farm in Erick.

He fell in love with country music, stole his first guitar, then opted to join the Army instead of going to jail for that theft. He was deployed to Korea to fight in 1952 and would later tell audiences, "I graduated from the Clash of '52!" His talent on the guitar and at songwriting sent him to Nashville, and the rest was history.

As for Wooley, he was actually the husband of Miller's cousin in Erick, and it was he who taught Miller how to play the guitar in the first place. Wooley himself was a songwriter, and he penned and sang a popular novelty song of the 1950s called "The [One-Eyed-One-Horned] Flying Purple Eater."

I mean you *must* visit a town that produced such an array of loony tunes, right? Wooley also put his acting chops on display, and he was on his way. His supporting role as an outlaw in the Gary Cooper film, *High Noon*, helped lead to his being cast as Pete Nolan in the popular *Rawhide* TV series.

The town of Erick features a single main street (Roger Miller Boulevard). At the point where that street intersects Sheb Wooley Avenue, there used to be museums, across the road from each other, dedicated to each of these entertainers. But I'm told they closed in 2017, and I'm glad I got to tour them before they did.

The historic Route 66 (the Mother Road) runs right through Erick, giving it more prominence. This was the road that so many "Okies" took to California during the Dust Bowl Days of Oklahoma. Erick flourished when Route 66 was the only way to get across that stretch of territory, but when Interstate 40 was built just north of the town, its boom days were largely over.

Erick sits on the western side of that formerly depressed, windswept area. The town is located only six miles east of the Texas panhandle border, in far western Beckham County. When I was there, the town's population was 1,000, and I doubt it's grown much since.

It could be any other two-stoplight town you might pass through, but I was drawn to-- well -- to the mystery or at least mystique of

Erick, Oklahoma. Although I'd never lived here, this place somehow seemed like home to me.

Have you ever encountered a place like that?

Maybe because it looked close to what the fictional town of Anarene, Texas, looked like in the film version of *The Last Picture Show*. It seemed to me that you have to be looking down Main Street at the right moment to really see any human activity on that main street. I was there in mid-day and didn't see much, anyway.

I felt compelled to drive around and see Erick, with its single street of commerce, and a half dozen porch-front neighborhoods, some with swings on those porches. It's obvious the town has been here awhile (1901, in fact, or six years before Oklahoma statehood) because the residential streets are graced with huge, statuesque Elm, Maple, and Blackjack trees. This latter ubiquitous batch sent me back to a childhood memory when I thought Blackjacks were the only trees in Oklahoma!

The town's mystique was enhanced in real life by the notorious killers Bonnie and Clyde in 1933. That's when Parker and Barrow kidnapped a couple Texas law enforcement officers, drove them to Erick at night, and left them tied to a tree, using barbed wire they cut from a farmer's fence. The bank robbers were long gone by the time the officers were freed from the tree.

Then there is the Sandhills Curiosity Shop, right there at 201 S. Sheb Wooley Avenue. Whatever tourists might come to Erick, this is the place they would probably talk about. This is where they would bring home some memorabilia of the town and Route 66.

For years, a sign on the front of the red brick store announces Erick to be "Redneck Capital of the World." The proprietors do not consider it a joke, but a proud statement of how they see the town.

The shop was created around 2010 by Harley and Annabelle Russell who moved to Erick from out of state and bought what was then the town's butcher shop. They felt the uniqueness of this town deserved something special that might help preserve what they saw as a town with "a rebellious, authentic musical soul."

Despite the shop's name, nothing is really for sale. Harley just loves tourists to take pictures and look at all the vintage commercial signs that adorn the building. He assures them they are all authentic relics of Americana. When you walk into this shop, you literally walk into a piece of American history from the early 20th Century.

A post on a Facebook page called "Il Mito Americano," (the American Myth), the writer describes the shop as, "A place out of time, brimming with Route 66 memorabilia, vinyl, old signs, books, pictures, weird and wonderful objects. But the real attraction is them: Harley and Annabelle, in quirky overalls and dresses, with their guitars and their country spirit, performed for travelers from every corner of the planet. They called themselves The Mediocre Music Makers – but trust me, they were anything but mediocre."

The post continues, "After Annabelle's disappearance in 2014, Harley has carried on solo. Today, opening that door (when it is available), you could experience a magical moment: a private performance, perhaps just for you, of the legendary *Get your kicks on Route 66*. That's what happened to us. Harley welcomed us bare-chested, in overalls, with his infectious smile and a unique energy. But it is also genuine, warm and deeply connected to Route 66."

Dreamer that I am, I wondered what it would be like to live here now. The thought was a pleasant one.

I didn't take that dream to far, though, because I knew I'd have just a smidgen of trouble selling the idea to my Kentucky wife, who had no reason to share my oneness with this town. Still, you just let some dreams settle into their own corners, no? Just let them settle in and become a little part of you. Kinda like my dad and his diner dream.

Still, maybe down the road if I find myself alone in life again and am just feeling like I'd like to get lost … I may return to Erick.

The University of Oklahoma Campus. Would it be the same, decades later?

15

Can We Go Home Again?

I can never go home again,
*   Never really find my town.*
*   — We Five (1964)*

Music has a great way of connecting us to our pasts, even though we may find our memories of home don't fit what we find when we return there years later.

As a college student, *We Five* was one of my favorite folk rock bands. When I say that, even some folks from my same era sometimes ask, "Who are *We Five*?"

I could tell you who they were in the 1960s, or who they were a few years ago when I became friends with one of its original members, Jerry Burgan, who is also seen as its co-founder. We both lived in Glendora, California, and hung out at the same guitar store, *Strings*.

Jerry agreed to have his revived group of We Five do a concert at the school where I was teaching, Azusa Pacific University. Most of the faces were different, but the sound was spot on. The APU students made a campus retro day out of it to honor the culture and feel of the 1960s.

The next year, I connected Jerry with a good Oklahoma friend, Joe Hight, who set up a concert for We Five at the University of Central Oklahoma. Joe and his wife Nan own a wonderful independent bookstore in Edmond called *Best of Books*. Sadly, Jerry died a couple years later in 2021.

If you don't recall We Five, you're probably not a baby boomer, unless you have heard your parents play their music. The band was a San Francisco folk/rock group (one of the first) founded by Michael Stewart (brother of the Kingston Trio's John Stewart) produced only one bonafide hit, nominated for a 1965 Grammy (Best Performance by a Vocal Group).

That song was a remake of one written by Ian and Sylvia, and it was, *You Were on My Mind*. If you're having trouble remembering it, just Google it. I loved the song but, over the course of a year, I also fell in love with almost every other song on the album of the same name.

A California friend of mine, Alan Rifkin who co-authored a book on We Five called *Wounds to Bind*, told me *You Were on my Mind* was, in his opinion, one of the best love songs of the folk-rock era.

The song that stuck in my mind and heart was another one called, *I Can Never Go Home Again*. You may not remember *that* one, but the excerpted lyrics above are from that song.

As the years passed, and I took flight from Oklahoma to start what I call my world tour of jobs, I thought about that song a lot. Seems like every time I'd pick up my guitar, I would be singing that song somewhere before I put it down. Still do, actually. Not just because it's a catchy tune, but because it deals with that issue of going home and wondering if it will be the same when and if you do.

I'm not just talking about going home to visit the folks or for a holiday reunion with friends and family. I'm talking about what happens when you let the memories of those good times and places sweep over you and lure you back home to live and work.

"It was such a great place, and I remember this little burger place near my college dorm," you say to yourself, often winding up with the question, "Wonder what it would be like to go back?"

I have tried going home twice as an adult, for different reasons and with different results.

The first time was in 1995 when I felt the need to return to my roots for a few months to recenter myself after a personal tragedy left me devastated. Ironically, on that occasion, my own pain encountered a far greater collective pain and tragedy that was the Oklahoma City bombing.

It was soothing to be surrounded by the familiar town and people, most notably Mom and Dad and my sister C.J., who did a lot of listening and gave me needed support.

Then, when the bombing occurred on April 19, I thrust myself back into my journalist's role that I had left a decade before for college teaching.

In that role, I was able to search for and provide answers to questions about the bombing, who was killed and injured, and how the recovery was going to the many people in Oklahoma who were craving such answers. That began to distract me from my own pain, and I felt I was in a community of others who were hurting. As I told their own stories of grief and recovery, I was also telling them my own.

I fell in love with the people of Oklahoma again, after so many years of trying to put distance between me and the state. I reported on the bombing's aftermath for a couple months and decided to move on with my life and career elsewhere. But that going-home experience put me on the road to personal recovery and healing.

Home in 2000

The second time was different. It was the fall of 2000, and my new wife Anne and I had just moved from our Memphis home and jobs, back to Norman, Oklahoma. I had accepted an endowed professorship at my alma mater, the University of Oklahoma.

Part of the reason for taking the job was the belief that, somehow, Norman would be the same wonderful college town that had provided me so many good experiences and memories as a student there in the 1960s. I realized I hadn't really seen the town since 1968, and I knew it might be somewhat different, but the allure was still strong enough to go.

Yes, there were differences with the town and with the campus. Both had grown and become more beautiful, but that didn't help me connect with the place I knew. And my old fraternity house was gone, maybe the target of Joni Mitchell's song, *They Paved Paradise and Put up a Parking Lot.* That hurt some.

The real differences, though, were in who my colleagues were and who I was myself.

In the 1960s, I had been a wide-eyed college student who dreamed the dreams all college kids do as they tried to make their grades so those dreams would come true. I was in the company of — and empathized with — the thousands of other students who were doing the same thing I was. Not to mention that it was all happening in the tumultuous counterculture decade of the 60s that seemed tailor-made for idealistic dreamers such as we.

The year 2000 posed a different scenario: I was no longer a student but a new faculty member in the company of absolutely no colleagues who lived the memories I had lived and, since most of them were not even from Oklahoma, didn't have the same attachment to OU that I had.

So, I was viewing "home" from a different perspective and through a different lens than I had three decades before as a student. Added to that, several of the faculty were in a cold war with each other for perceived wrongs. In some cases, they were acting more immaturely than I remembered us college students acting years before. In hindsight, though, that statement may be a stretch.

Nevertheless, within the first three months, I concluded that this was not the home I had remembered it to be. Anne was finding her own work over the School of Dance to be more than she had bargained for, so we decided to pull up stakes at the end of the school year and head back to the University of Memphis.

We had only been gone from there a year, and we knew this time that things couldn't have changed *that* much.

Or could they?

Workers comb through the rubble of the Alfred P. Murrah Federal Building.
Jim Willis

16

A Day Unlike Any Other

A folk music group from the 1990s, "Cry, Cry, Cry," released an enigmatic song called *Shades of Gray* in 1998 written by Dar Williams. The lyrics follow three young men from Arkansas on their misguided road trip in 1995, full of mischief and entry-level crime, through the backroads of Arkansas, Kansas, and Oklahoma.

It seems a straightforward folk tale until the three guys cross the Oklahoma line. But it turns darker, flashing a stunning revelation, late in the song. I nearly fell out of my seat when I heard it, because it brought back one of the most important times in my life.

Memories return

I remember when I first heard *Shades of Gray* in the year of its release, because it took me back to April, 1995. That was when I hit life's clutch and downshifted into low gear to pull myself back into my sane lane. I was still hurting badly from the loss of my wife and, three years later, this ballad took me back to my 1995 stopover in my native Oklahoma City, on my cross-country road trip to recenter myself.

It brought back with shocking clarity how stunned I was when I heard the news of what happened on the Wednesday morning of April 19 as I ate breakfast in suburban OKC.

The Jimmy's Egg diner was full of breakfast patrons, and my brother in law Ben and I were at a corner table chatting away over our omelets and grits. All of a sudden, the tile floor beneath our feet jolted, the walls around us shook for a split second, and we heard a muffled boom!

A moment later a TV news bulletin flashed across the screen, announcing there had been an explosion at the Alfred P. Murrah Federal Building in downtown Oklahoma City.

What happened?

The immediate speculation was an exploded natural gas line. It happened just after most of the offices opened for business at 9 a.m., and there may be injuries involved, the news anchor said.

This would be the first of an endless string of news updates over the next several days but, at this point, the cause and damage were unknown.

Within a few minutes, videocams were on the scene at the Federal Building, and the footage was devastating. The foreground was littered with dozens of charred, burned-out cars, some still on fire and others smoldering. Running, staggering, and hobbling through this carnage were an untold number of people trying to escape the burning building.

Tragic images

Firefighters in full gear were dragging hoses and pick axes toward the rubble; police officers were trying to set up barriers and string yellow caution tape around the area, and nurses and doctors trying to tend to victims on the spot, whether that be the middle of the parking lot or on the grassy lawns away from the building.

But what caught your attention even more was the still-standing, yet mortally wounded hulk of this 9-story brick Federal Building, with most of its façade gone along with a mammoth, semi-circular crevice from the front side of the building.

You could stare straight into the bowels of this carcass and see what was left of the upper floors and then, as your eyes scanned down to earth, the flattened, pancakes stack of concrete floors piled on top of each other.

Godzilla's bite

It was as if Godzilla had stomped into downtown Oklahoma City, reached down and taken a huge bite out of a 9-layer cookie wafer and spit the pieces out into the surrounding streets.

As the news cameras panned around to the surrounding streets, you could see that neighboring buildings failed to escape the wrath of the Murrah Building explosion.

Taking much of the punch were the Athenian Building, the Water Resources Board Building, the Journal-Record Building, and the Downtown YMCA, all lined up on Northwest 5th Street facing the Federal Building just across the street to the south.

Remembering the Y

Watching the screen, my gaze hung on the YMCA for a moment, realizing that was where I had spent so many hours swimming with the Boy Scouts when I was young and earning all the Red Cross life-saving badges plus – in later years – my SCUBA diving certification. The building was ripped apart and would undoubtedly have to be imploded.

Ten minutes later, the newscasters had amended their earlier speculation about a gas line explosion and were calling this the result of a bombing by persons unknown. Also amended was the conservative estimate of a few people injured; now the reality had set in that many people were not only injured but also killed.

Some still trapped

Some were still trapped inside the rubble, and rescue efforts had begun. Then the sobering announcement was made that that second floor of the Federal Building housed not only offices, but a working day care center that had been fully populated with children and toddlers.

Newscasters soon began issuing pleas for viewers to give blood at their local Red Cross donor sites, and to buy and drop off needed emergency supplies. Everything was needed downtown, from bottled water, to first-aid supplies, to batteries, to blankets ... to diapers. Numerous drop-off locations were available for these volunteered items. Ben and I left the diner and see what we could to help.

Trying to help

He headed toward Walmart and I went to find the Red Cross Blood Donation Center in Norman. When I arrived, there was already a long line forming. On this day, if you were in or near Oklahoma City, you wanted desperately to do even your small bit to help. Twenty minutes later, I was in the donor room, having my blood typed, tested.

After the blood center, I headed toward Walmart, finding many of the shelves already empty, but picking up some items I thought could be useful at the bombing site.

Throughout the day the continuous news reports showed the gravity of the situation downtown. The casualty count was climbing, hour by hour, and estimates were it could reach as high as 100 or more dead and upwards to 1,000 injured.

168 dead

The final death count, which wouldn't be known for days, was 168. More than 800 were injured.

Not all those casualties were from the Murrah Building itself. Many of the injured were from those either outside on surrounding sidewalks and streets, or they were from the buildings that ringed the Federal Building. Flying glass, along with the debris blasting through those windows, found their mark on those going about their Wednesday morning's work.

Throughout the day, nearly everyone in the Oklahoma City area was multi-tasking: doing their day jobs while also listening to news updates on radio or TV. The picture was starting to become a little clearer as the day went on. At 9:02 a.m. a person or persons had exploded what looked like a huge homemade bomb at the Murrah Building. The first day's investigation showed it had been placed in a Ryder rental truck, parked at the front entrance of the building.

American terrorists

The initial thought was that it was a terrorism act probably committed by Middle Easterners. The memory of the 1993 attack on the World Trade Center in New York City was still on the country's mind. It happened shortly after noon on February 26 when a blast erupted from the parking garage beneath the trade center and carved out a crater almost 100 feet across.

It only took a day to realize this was not the work of Middle Eastern terrorists but of a home-grown pair of disgruntled Americans, Timothy McVeigh and Terry Nichols, who resorted to terrorism out of revenge for the AFT and FBI raid on the Branch Davidian compound in Waco, Texas. April 19, 1995, was the two-year anniversary of that raid.

Years later, on Jan. 6, 2020, I would watch a large throng of right-wing extremists attack the nation's Capitol. I wondered then, as I do now,, if any of them or their supporters realized they were engaging in the same kind of crazed reaction that Timothy McVeigh did when he pulled the trigger on the Murrah Federal Building on April 19, 1995.

Would they have supported McVeigh's actions?

Back to the streets

As the sun went down on this day of infamy, I was exhausted emotionally but I still felt a driving need to help in whatever way I could.

It had been a few years since I'd worked full-time as a professional journalist, having turned to teaching the craft at Boston College. But my skills were still intact, and I knew everyone was hungry for answers to what had happened on this day and why.

I decided to return to the streets of Oklahoma City as a reporter gathering those answers. After reporting and writing two dozen stories over the next few weeks, I realized it was the best decision I'd ever made.

Helping others had, in turn, helped to heal me and put my own personal pain in perspective. Reporting on the determination of my fellow Sooners to move beyond the pain and danger that befell Oklahoma City had convinced me I could still summon up the strength to make positive contributions to life as well.

(This is adapted from my 2025 book, *The Long Pivot Home.*)

Skip Fernandez and his Aspen, just off a
night searching the rubble pile.
Jim Willis

17

A Play Drive and a Prey Drive

Among the many heroes who emerged from the ashes of the Oklahoma City bombing in April, 1995, were three Golden Retrievers from Miami, Florida, with the unlikely names of *Aspen, Maggie, and Brandee.*

The dogs all belonged to the Metro Dade County Fire Department and were also a part of the FEMA Task Force 1 from Miami. All three were trained search-and-rescue dogs, and all performed brilliantly.

I met all of them and was instantly smitten. I fell in love on the spot with Aspen.

The dogs of gold

Fire departments around the country use Golden Retrievers, as well as a few other breeds, to locate missing children and to find the bodies of victims often buried under piles of rubble.

Such was the case when domestic terrorists blew apart the Alfred P. Murrah Federal Building on the morning of April 19, 1995.

These and other rescue dogs sniffed, climbed, and dug their way through the tons of debris left in the wake of that bombing. Over eight days, Aspen, Maggie, and Brandee scampered unleashed over tall, dangerous rubble piles and into tight, hidden voids that led to canyons beneath the cluttered surface to find many bodies that human searchers could not find themselves.

Risky work

Their work was dangerous, because parts of the 9-story building were still standing precariously, as torched and bent steel girders and cables, that could break at any minute, were the only things keeping the remaining structure from caving in on the rubble below.

All the bent, twisted, and fallen pieces of the Murrah Building were very much like a giant Jenga tower. Knocking down or even jostling the wrong piece could cause the whole remaining structure to collapse on anyone — human or canine — below.

Covering the story

I was a journalist covering this search-and-rescue operation, and to say I was impressed with what I saw and heard about these dogs, would be a gross understatement. They were wonderful.

The first fireman I interviewed was Miami's Skip Fernandez, who was sitting on a curb across the street from the building's carcass. A beautiful brown-eyed Golden Retriever named Aspen was sitting between his splayed-out legs. Both of them looked very tired and very sad.

Skip looked like he wanted to talk, so I sat down to listen. Aspen never took her eyes off me, even when I took her picture.

"Golden Retrievers have a natural propensity to be drawn to people," Skip said. "And that is highly important, because these dogs have to have an affinity for people. It must be strong enough for them to want to seek people out and help them if possible."

Skip and Aspen had just come off a 13-hour shift on the Murrah rubble pile, searching for any signs of life — or any dead bodies. There would be plenty of the latter before the search was over: 168 perished in this bombing. More than 600 were injured, many severely.

The 2-year-old Aspen was the embodiment of a well-trained rescue dog who had the natural instincts and traits needed for the job. And, when off-duty, she served another purpose as a great *stress-reliever* for many of the human first-responders who worked the disaster scene.

Aspen and the other dogs transitioned quickly to the role of therapy dogs for those searchers traumatized by all that they saw and experienced on the remains of the Murrah Building.

"The crews really enjoy these dogs and play around with them a lot after work," Skip said. "The dogs help take the guys' minds off what they have just seen in the rubble pile. And the dogs love those playtimes, too."

For Skip himself, Aspen represented a new love in his life, and she replaced a painful loss.

"I lost a Golden Retriever to cancer last year, and it was just like losing one of my daughters," he remembered. "Her name was Sierra, and she was 11 when she died. Now I have Aspen, and I love her. She lives with me and, when she leaves the department, she will be retired to my backyard."

The dogs are recruited from all parts of the country. Aspen came as a puppy from the Sunjoie Kennels in Topanga, California. Skip said the fire department likes to get the dogs as puppies and take them through a process of bonding, socialization, and training.

Specifically, fire departments look for two inborn traits or drives: These are what they call the *"prey drive"* and the *"play drive."*

"The dogs have to be natural hunters and love hunting," he said. "But they also have to love to play, because that is the reward we give them for doing a good job."

In Oklahoma City, when the dogs' 12-hour shifts were over, they would be taken to the nearby Myriad Botanical Gardens. There, for 90 minutes, they could run, chased balls or frisbees, play with firemen, roll in the grass and generally enjoy themselves.

Fernandez called it, "Their de-stressor time."

Then the dogs would be taken to the Myriad Convention Center where the firemen were housed, and there they would get a well-deserved sleep until it was time to head back to the rubble pile for more work.

"These dogs actually turned hours into minutes," Fernandez said. "And they located many victims we would have never found otherwise."

Despite the dangers from falling debris and precarious footing on the rubble, none of them were injured or suffered any serious cuts. He attributed much of that to the dogs' exhaustive training in working under simulated conditions.

Asked how Aspen performed, Skip beamed and said, "She got an A!"

Metro Dade Fire Department is one of a network of departments around the country who contribute their human and canine first responders to the Federal Emergency Management Administration

(FEMA). When disasters occur anywhere in the country, they can be called into action.

Eleven FEMA teams like Skip's came to Oklahoma City instantly for a two-week period of search and rescue. Most of them brought dogs like Aspen. Although Golden Retrievers make up only one-third of Metro Dade's K-9 Rescue Teams (the other nine are Labs, German Shepherds, and Malimois) they made up 100 percent of the three dogs that came to Oklahoma City. All were females.

It seems somehow ironic that gentle dogs like Aspen, Maggie, and Brandee who have such a natural love for people — especially children — are the ones who are often assigned to locating the lost and dead ones. And yet, maybe it is only right that they do.

Still, there was an undeniable sadness in Aspen's eyes on the morning when we first met. She seemed to know exactly what was going on.

(Aspen has since passed away but spent her last years living with Skip, who rose in the ranks of the Miami-Dade Fire Department and then retired.)

18

A Horse Named Star

In April 1995, as I've noted before, I found myself in Oklahoma, reporting on the aftermath of the Murrah Federal Building bombing, and not knowing what tomorrow would bring.

I certainly did not expect it to bring a very different kind of relationship into my life, but it did.

Looking for distractions from the pain we all felt – and the personal pain I felt from losing my wife, I decided to drive south from Norman to Ardmore, about an hour's drive, on a sunny

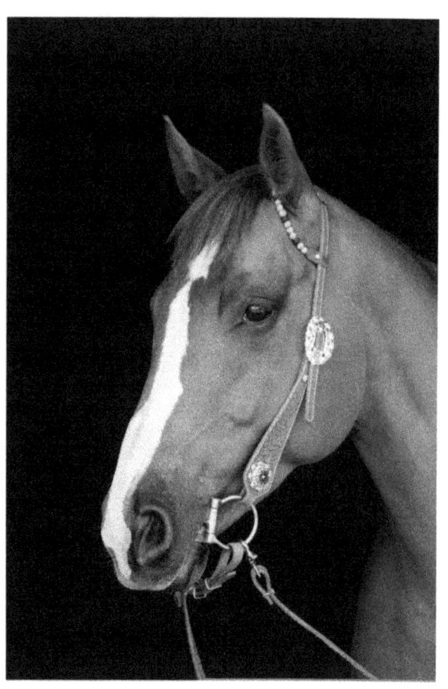

There are few animals as elegant as a Quarter Horse. Mine was named Star.
Rebecca's Pictures/Pixabay

Saturday morning in early April and check out a horse breeders auction.

Even though I grew up in horse country, in a town where the Shetland Pony became a familiar sight because of a popular pony farm there, I had never attended a horse breeders auction. I was certainly not thinking of buying a horse, but I thought it would be enjoyable to see some of the finest horses in Oklahoma and Texas strut their stuff in the arena as buyers bid for the steeds.

Had I just gone into the arena, taken a seat, and enjoyed the sale for a couple hours, it would have been a pleasant-enough day. Just not the great one it turned out to be.

Arriving before the auction began, I veered off into the barn where the neatly bathed and groomed horses awaited their moment in the sale ring. As I walked the sawdust aisle past the stalls, I realized I'd never seen so many beautiful animals in one place before.

The horses all began to blend into one continual blur, like a LeRoy Neiman painting, until I came to the last stall on the left and a two-year-old Quarter Horse mare bearing the hip number of 153. Her name was Star, and I was struck instantly. Her sorrel coat was so fine and smooth, three of her legs bore gleaming white socks, her ears stood at attention, and it was all topped off by a white lopsided blaze smack in the middle of her face, and just between two of the softest brown eyes that seemed to peer right into my soul. In the vernacular of equine enthusiasts, Star sported a lot of chrome.

"How would you like to come with me, big girl?" I found myself asking her.

She didn't say no. To me, the deal was sealed at that point.

To the uninitiated, a Quarter Horse is a well-built animal bred for speed, and reputed to be the fastest horse over a quarter-mile. She certainly sent my heart racing on this April day.

It was love at first sight and, I knew she was exactly what I wanted. She could make the pain go away, in time. Would she be expensive? Yes. Did I care? At that point, no. I reasoned, if you can call it that, I had just lost a beautiful woman, so why pass up this opportunity to share my life with a beautiful equine? Expense is one thing, but the value that a purchase like Star could add to my life could be, well, invaluable.

It would be several hours before we could ride off to the sunset, though, because she wasn't scheduled to show until late afternoon. And, of course, I had no idea how much I'd have to pay to make this new dream a reality. Nor, for that matter, did I have a trailer to get her back to Norman. Nor did I have a place to put her back in Norman. And, oh right: I had no real cash on me. But I did have a brand new Master Card with a $6,000 balance.

I would need all of it.

I went back into the sale arena and sat on my hands while horse after horse went up for auction, afraid I might get impulsive and be tempted to bid on a lesser candidate before Star.

As I sat through this parade, I realized this wasn't the first time I had lost a woman and opted to go forward in life with a horse instead. It had been my senior year at the University of Oklahoma: 1968. I had been dating Susan for some time, and was so sure we would be married, that I cobbled together enough cash to surprise her with an engagement ring.

I took her to dinner for the formal proposal and was so sure she would spill her soup in her rush to spit out "YES!", that I didn't even notice when she said "*No*".

After a few seconds of a reality check, my words came: "Not sure I heard that right, Sue. Once more, please?" After all, since "no" can sound so much like "yes," I thought I'd better check, and this time I heard the subtle distinction. For a couple reasons, the kind that don't make much sense to anyone beyond 21, she had -- in fact -- said no.

Although I've been eternally grateful since then that she did so, it took a while for my sanity to set in and displace my shock and awe that night. But we made it through the dessert, and I took her home. Then I went home, talked it out with my big sister, went to bed and had a good night's sleep.

When dawn broke, I decided to push forward. Zales would not take the ring back, so I decided to trade it for something that caught my eye earlier in the week: a horse named Shorty. Surely this kind of relationship would be easier to handle, and everyone knows how loyal your horse can be.

Everything was going okay until the next evening when Susan called to tell me she *maaay* have been a bit too hasty with the "no." Looked like she may want me and the ring, after all. I was about to ask if she would settle for a horse instead because that's what the ring had morphed into, but I took the high road and said, "Let's think about that, Sue. This day has been rainy, and maybe you're just overly depressed right now."

The subject was never revisited.

As I've taught Interpersonal Communication in college over the years, I have sometimes suggested that students use a line like that when they want their "no" to glide down easily. It certainly worked well for Susan and me and allowed us to have much better lives than a hasty "yes" would have handed us.

Back to Star, waiting eagerly in the barn to start a new life with me. It was approaching 5 p.m., and she was one of the last horses to enter the sale ring that Saturday afternoon. Watching her go through her paces, I resolved that no one was going to separate me from this magnificent animal.

The bidding began, and it was lively. A half-dozen of us were battling at the start but, after a series of $100 and $200 bumps, I leap-frogged a thousand over the last bid, and there were only two of us left. Another thousand later, and there was just one.

Star and I were now a twosome, my Master Card was on fire and melted out of shape, and I figured out the rest of the logistics before nightfall.

From that point on, this horse and rider spent several years happily exploring the hills and trails of Oklahoma and, later, Tennessee and -- then again -- back to Oklahoma for a year. She seemed to make it her mission to get me over the hurdles I faced. I like to think I did the same for her.

More immediately, in these few short months spent in reunion with Oklahoma that spring and summer, I stabled Star a couple miles south of Norman and I would see and ride her daily after driving back from the bomb site. She was a lifesaver on many of those days, lifting my spirits and reminding me that life is not all tragic and that even a horse named Star can bring a shot of sunlight back to my days.

I would move on to a new teaching assignment at the University of Memphis that summer, but I took Star with me, and we remained a team for years to come.

(Part of this chapter is an adaptation of material from my book, The Long Pivot Home.)

19

A Farewell in Oklahoma City

The author in front of the carcass of the Murrah Building, 1995.

The search for bodies at the Alfred P. Murrah Federal Building in Oklahoma City came to an official end on May 10, 1995 when searchers came as close as they would to extracting all known bodies from the devastation. The final death toll from the April 19 bombing was 60 people fewer than the 228 that officials had feared were dead.

When the search ended that Thursday night, firefighters from Oklahoma City and eleven FEMA teams had pulled 164 bodies from the rubble, and 18 of them were children. Two adult bodies would never be found, Chief Jon Hansen said, and two more would die later from critical injuries sustained on the day of the bombing. Then there were the known injuries that numbered at least 645 victims.

"It's a miracle all but two of the dead were found," Hansen told our gathering of reporters in a midnight briefing. "But we have compared lists with the medical examiner, and are down to two out of the entire number of people lost. It's a sad relief, however. They (searchers) did it for the victims' families, for their communities, and for the state."

With the search over, the remains of the Murrah Building were turned over to police and FBI agents to continue their search for clues as to how the blast actually occurred and to gather more evidence for coming trials of the perpetrators. After that, the General Services Administration (GSA) was to get the building, and it would be their final decision to demolish it. There was some discussion of preserving the structure and restoring it, but polls were taken that showed 68 percent of Oklahoma City respondents favored tearing it down and building a permanent memorial on the site. Eventually, that's what would happen.

On Friday, May 11, a final on-site memorial was held at 2 p.m. in memory of the victims and in thanks for those who came from near and far to help rescue those who could be rescued, and search for the bodies of those who could not. I covered that story, and I will never forget what was uncharted territory for me as I reported on this outdoor memorial service, held on and around the rubble of the Murrah Building. It was also meant to be a show of gratitude for all the many first-responders from Oklahoma City and around the nation who came to help in the mammoth search-and-rescue operation. Another body had been found from the day before, leaving only one known body, a nurse who was still unaccounted for despite the best efforts of the search teams.

I showed up early for the service, and it was the first time most of the reporters were allowed to stand on the building's site. It was no longer deemed an active crime scene, and the building was set to be imploded a few days later, although there would be at least one delay before that was done.

My own emotional firewall I had erected three weeks ago had cracked a couple of times since then, and it would fall later this day. I could feel it coming when I stood on the building's bricks and mortar under a beautiful Friday afternoon sun. I had brought my Minolta 35mm camera along with a telephoto lens, and it helped immensely as I scanned the wide area looking for individual vignettes, facial expressions, or artifacts that would speak more voluminously than a thousand words. I wrote about them in the story that follows.

I knew there was a formal program planned as a stage and dais had been erected at the base of the building on which the Oklahoma governor and mayor of Oklahoma City would speak, along with others. But I also knew that the story I was going to tell would have nothing to do with those formalities or what might be said. Upon arriving, I knew instinctively that my goal was simply to bring my readers to this scene to see, hear, and feel some of what this rubble and these many mourners had to say simply by their presence and demeanor. It was going to be a story based almost totally on my observations of what lay out in front of me and memories of all I had seen and heard since the day of the bombing. Frankly, I didn't know where to begin.

I knew I had time to work it out, though, because this was Friday afternoon, today's paper had already gone to press, and the Sun had no Saturday edition. So, this story would be for Sunday, and deadline wasn't until tomorrow afternoon. Still I wanted to write it while everything I saw, heard, and felt were still fresh. After the memorial service ended, I walked hurriedly to my car, parked a couple blocks away.

Along that short route, nearly a month after the Murrah bomb had gone off, after all the days and weeks of witnessing the carnage at ground zero, all the while dealing with feelings of personal loss, my emotional dam broke. I was at my SUV, and I remember reaching out for the door handle, and then freezing in place while the tears flooded out. I leaned into the still-closed car door for support and just let my feelings out. The whole scene probably took less than a minute, but it seemed longer. The tears ceased about as abruptly as they had begun, but it was the cathartic moment I needed.

As I entered the car and sat down in the driver's seat, I instinctively pulled my cell phone from my jeans to call my former wife just as I used to do after I had experienced any impactful event. While dialing her number though, the reality hit me hard that she, of course, was no longer a part of my life. So I hung up and called my sons and then my parents. I told Min and Kao that I loved them and what I was feeling at the moment about the tragedy I was covering. I told them we all needed to work to make sure nothing like this ever happened again, and they agreed and said they were with me in spirit.

"Hi Mom, this is me and I just called to say I love you," I began. "I'm at the site of the bombing, and I had this overwhelming need to call you and Dad and tell you how sad I was about all I had just witnessed. Then I told them how much I loved them.

Mom waited and responded, "I hear you Jim, and I love you, too. Papa and I have been watching, and we can't imagine what it's like for you, being right there at the scene. But I agree it can never happen again."

I felt better after letting my emotions out and connecting with my family that day. Then I turned the car toward Norman and my apartment to begin writing about what I had witnessed this afternoon. I couldn't wait to get to my Mac and start writing.

Once there, I launched into the story with all the zeal and adrenalin a writer feels when they know they have a story that must be written and they know it deserves a unique way of being written. I was glad that I would have a lot of time to collect my thoughts and rewrite the first drafts, because the *Sun* did not publish on Saturday, my deadline wasn't until the next afternoon (Saturday). As it turns out, I would not need the extra time.

On my drive to Norman, the afternoon sky had turned dark and it was raining hard now. As I sat down and began to write my story, I heard the first claps of thunder and saw a couple patented Oklahoma lightning streaks. Interesting background noise for such an electric story, I thought. The story wrote itself virtually as my observations, memories, and feelings coalesced into words that spread across the screen like soft butter spreads across warm toast. I was about five pages into the story, with the finish line in sight, when one of those lightning bolts hit the roof of my building and my Mac screen went instantly dark. This was the time before built-in surge protectors and automatic saves.

When I restarted the computer, my story was gone.

I sat there and stared at the blank screen, let out a loud moan and more than one "Shit!" but then regrouped and challenged myself to mentally recoup what I had just written.

As a professor of journalism, I've lost track of the number of "my-dog-ate-my-story" excuses students parried when they missed a deadline. But ever since this experience of losing my own story, in which I just started typing again and wrote what I think was an even better story, I am deaf to those student excuses.

"Then why didn't you just turn around and write it again?" I ask those students.

I submitted my story to my editor Carol Hartzog the next day, and I was not at all sure she wouldn't ask for a major rewrite, because this piece was told so unconventionally. One of the liberating things about writing a good story is that the form just seems to take its own shape as you move along. Writers sometimes speak of "opening a vein" as they pour their blood into a story.

Former *Baltimore Sun* reporter Jon Franklin, who won a Pulitzer Prize for a story about a woman battling cancer, recalled John Steinbeck talking about the feeling of holding "fire in my hands" when his writing is hitting the mark.

"I never knew what that meant," Franklin said. "[But] I started reading [my story] through and I noticed that my heart was racing. The piece was having a physiological effect on me. Whatever the hell it was, it was a moment you do not forget when you get a feeling from your own piece. God it was fun."

This is exactly how I felt writing this memorial story. It was having this kind of emotional effect on me, although I wouldn't call it fun. But it was what good writers are in the business for: to tell an important story in a way that will bring the reader to the scene. For this story, I was guided by the fresh memories of what I had witnessed, and my goal was simple: I wanted to bring my reader to the scene; to *see and feel* what we all were seeing and feeling.

My subconscious seemed to take over and glided me through the writing process and, when I was finished and looked back over the draft, I was surprised to see I'd written much of it in the second person. That was something I'd never done before, it was against a basic rule of Journalism 101 to stay in the third person, but I felt it hit my goal of allowing others to see what I had seen. I guess Carol saw that, too, because she approved it with no edits at all.

Here is how that story, headlined with a simple **Farewell**, read:

You stand on Fifth Street in the shadow of what once was the Alfred P. Murrah Federal Building. The sun bathes the scene, and there is an official ceremony underway, but that story is dwarfed by what your eyes take in as you look around.

You can't take those eyes off the nine-story carcass in front of you and how it is affecting the many who have gathered here.

Hundreds of search-and-rescue workers come to pay their respects. They remember those 168 who died inside its walls, including the two women's bodies, yet unrecovered, and nurse Rebecca Anderson who lost her life after heroic attempts to rescue victims children from the building.

Six of those lost are still unidentified.

And they remember the many who did so much in trying to save the savable and locate the lost.

On Saturday, it would be the survivors and victims' families who would be doing on-site remembering. They would each be given a rose and allowed to pick up a piece of the rubble and take it home.

They would be allowed to meet individually with Gov. Frank Keating and then continue their mourning at the First Christian Church. It would be a much more private ceremony and run longer than this public, 10-minute rite.

But on this Friday, it was time for the rescuers, volunteers, and even journalists to remember and to mourn.

You look up and see this monument of man's inhumanity to man, it's hollowed-out section of floors, and the rubble pile remaining below. Yet you also know you are staring straight into a tower of love and self-sacrifice. You think instantly of the Oklahoma City police and firefighters as typified by Gary Marrs, Jon Hansen, and Sam Gonzales.

You think also of far-away firemen like Miami's Angel Machado, Capt. Greg Gerlach, and Skip Fernandez with his wonderful Golden Retriever, Aspen. The dogs like Aspen could have been anyone's backyard pets, but they were born to a greater mission of search and rescue, and they acquitted themselves brilliantly here.

Everywhere you look you see flowers, wreaths, teddy bears, and hand-painted signs of thanks. A rose juts its dark red head out of an orange highway cone wrapped in duct tape that looks like it has been kicked more than once by a frustrated rescuer. Another rose dangles from the tripod belonging to a Reuters news photographer.

Elsewhere, two fatigues-clad National Guardsmen – like many of their comrades, -- bow their heads and clutch rose stems behind their backs. An FBI agent does the same.

There are those who insist that, in the battle between the eye and the ear, the eye wins every time. That seems true here today. There is so much to see, so much to take in. There is so much to remember for fear that – if you don't – you may forget your resolve to hate violence in any form.

You realize this is the legacy of violence.

Still, if you let your ears take over for a moment, you can hear the sound of bagpipes coming from somewhere down front, near the rubble pile ... near the infamous crater the bomb created. The strained music of the pipes seems a fitting memorial to those who lived and died and tried here.

If you can pull your eyes from the sight in front of you and pivot north, you see another moving image. In a blown-out window frame from five floors up in the Journal-Record Building, you see a team of hatless hardhats taking a break from clean-up and repair duties. They cluster shoulder to shoulder and lean out the space, gazing at the scene just south of them, across Fifth Street. They gaze at the Murrah Building's remains. They seem like men with hard jobs, but at this moment they are thinking very soft thoughts.

If you let your imagination wander as you survey that Journal-Record Building, with its windowless walls and top floor opening to the sky, you can almost hear it whispering to the federal building. It could be consoling its friend saying "I understand. I hurt, too. That was one hell of a blast, wasn't it?"

The same might be heard from the Downtown Y, standing just to the east of the federal building. Eleven million dollars. That was the Y's damage estimate. Like the 19 children who perished in the Murrah rubble, the Y stands as a symbol of innocence vastly underserving of such a fate. If ever there were a tribute to more peaceful things in life it is that YMCA.

You think to yourself, "I used to swim there as a child when I was in the Boy Scouts." But what you see now is a darkened cavern inside with headlamps of workers peering out, and miles of plywood windows blocking out the sun from this once-happy building.

Looking up again at the Murrah Building, you see spray-painted numbers everywhere, identifying the remaining columns. There is a gap between columns 20 and 22, where 24 once stood. This is the building's chief crater where so many of the innocents died.

You see the bracings put in place to keep the tilting columns from falling or caving in and bringing much of the remaining building down with them. Reporters were told earlier in the week that the entire east wall had tilted outward 28 inches since the April 19 blast. Oklahoma winds can do that.

As your eyes scan the floors and columns, you realize you are looking at a giant, hand-painted grid. You think of the grid paper you used back in high school drafting classes. But you know these grids signify missing structures; not planned ones. As you continue looking, your eyes are drawn into the remaining office spaces themselves, now open to the great outdoors. The walls are gone. You see rows of heaving filing cabinets, desks, coat racks, and rows of book cases. Some things have been untouched by the bomb. But, on the other side of an office, there is a hole where nothing at all exists. Your eyes pan downward and you can see the crushed debris below. And you can only imagine, in horror, that all of that would have fallen on the trapped humans below.

You remember the one terrific briefing where columns 20 and 22 of the Murrah Building were described, and of why they figured so prominently in the danger to searchers plowing through the rocks below.

You look at the sections of missing floors up above and remember the story of the man picking up his Social Security check and of the clerk reaching across the counter to give it to him. He lived, she died. And you realize that, on Wednesday, April 19, at 9:02 a.m., life or death for some was a matter of which side of the office floor you were standing on.

You recall first-responders like Jon Hansen saying how much the FEMA teams had waned to stay on the job past today and see it through to its end. Now, without any doubt, you understand why they feel that way.

After all, straight ahead in your line of vision is the pile of floors pancaked on tops of each other. And in between the first and second floor slabs were the bodies of 19 children in the Murrah Building daycare center.

And you pray fervently that no one will ever see anything like this again.

In reading through my story, I realized this had been an opportunity to reflect with the readers about much of what had occurred in the few short weeks since the Murrah Building exploded. And I was gratified when a woman wrote a note to me after reading the story.

It said simply, "Thank you, Mr. Willis. Your story made me feel like I was there at that memorial."

Since that was my intent in writing it the way I did, her comment reminded me that what I was doing was worthwhile. It was also an experience that writers crave: having the privilege to latch on to a story that tests you in every way possible and to feel you have applied your talents well to the challenge. It would not be for another year that I would come across writer Jon Franklin's comment about a writer's "holding fire in your hands," but – when I did read that – I realized that was exactly what I had done with the *Farewell* story. I had now been a journalist or journalism instructor for nearly three decades, and it had never been more exhilarating than it was after covering the Oklahoma City bombing.

After the *Farewell* story was written, there was only one major ground-zero assignment remaining for me, although most of the nation's journalistic core had pulled out and gone home a week or more earlier. I was still struck by their absence, because the story of how Oklahoma was recovering from this mass murder was much more than a body-count story. But I also understand the economics of the news business and the fact that, if it's not an event playing in your backyard, your station management wants you home covering those events that are. It's just not worth the expense of having you cover "someone else's news."

But there was still one major story yet to come, and that was the planned demolition of the Murrah Building, only a few days away. It would be delayed for weather and technical reasons until May 23, but Carol Hartzog assigned me that story and, as the day approached, I wondered how I would meaningfully fill this gaping hole on Page 1 that was reserved for the story of an event that would take only a few seconds to complete from start to finish.

On the night of May 22, I decided to go down to Satellite City, look at the Murrah Building on the eve of its destruction, and – strange as it sounds – see if it could be my muse and show me how to frame this story. When I arrived at the parking lot about 9 p.m., there were no other reporters around. I was glad, because I didn't want any distractions as I contemplated tomorrow's story. I knew that if the implosion were delayed an hour or two, I would be on a short deadline. Maybe I could even write some background material for the story tonight and just top it off tomorrow after the blast was done.

It was a warm evening, and I got out of my car, sat on the hood, and stared up at the remains of the building. I'm not sure how long I just sat there looking and remembering all that had happened over the past three weeks. At some point, it occurred to me that this building was not very old. Then, as I looked around to the neighboring structures, I realized the Murrah Building was like the new kid on the block. I decided to research the origins of the building later that night when I got home, and a frame for the story began forming in my mind.

I arrived at the implosion scene about 6 a.m. on Tuesday. The blast was to occur promptly at 7 a.m., and I was ready for it. I was one of a battalion of reporters and photojournalists who were standing in Satellite City, waiting for the go-moment. The charge exploded on schedule, and the Murrah Building crumbled before our eyes, landing in a heap of dust and smoke within a few seconds. It was over almost before it began. I turned to go back to my car, and head to the paper to write the story. But my focus was diverted by a young police officer in the same parking lot who stood by his squad car, just staring intently at the rubble... I was curious, so I decided to walk over and chat with him.

"Good morning, officer," I said. "I'm Jim Willis, a reporter for the *Edmond Evening Sun*, and I see you had the same idea I did about getting one last look at her."

He turned and smiled, and I was grateful he didn't just bark orders at me to leave him alone.

"Right. This sort of falls into the weirdness category," Barnett said. " I hate to see it fall. There's a strange attachment to this building."

"I agree," I said. "I have felt that, too, over the past few weeks."

It turns out, Barnett was one of the police officers on-site the morning of the bombing, and he said it was horrible working the northwest corner of the building where few survived. I could tell he was still envisioning what happened the morning of April 19 and, like

Skip Fernandez who I met on my first day of coverage, Barnett seemed like he wanted to talk about it.

He told me he had actually been sitting in his squad car all night, just staring at the building's carcass. I didn't want to rush him, though, so we just stood there looking up at rubble. Then, quietly and pensively, he broke the silence.

"I was here from the beginning," he said, still staring at where the building had stood. "I think about that day of April 19. I think about the two bodies still inside the rubble. I would have given anything just to have found one person alive that morning. I keep thinking, what if there were a way to undo it? I drive by that building all the time. What if one of us had seen him and stopped him?"

At 7:10 a.m. J.W. Barnett stood alone by his squad car, staring into the void at Fifth and Robinson.

"It's done," he said.

I asked if I could quote him, and he said yes. So, Officer Barnett wound up in my story that day, and I often wonder how he has dealt with his memories over the years since the morning of April 19, 1995.

As for my story itself, the framing that I feel the building itself gave me the night before was the one I went with. And if I thought my memorial story of a few days before was unconventional, this one probably topped it. Once again I was surprised that Carol approved it and didn't ask for a rewrite.

The story began this way:

Amid an immediate family of much older siblings, the teenager died just after dawn today.

Mortally wounded by assassins' explosives a month ago, the Alfred P. Murrah Federal Building was finished off by less than 150 pounds of charges that were detonated about 7 a.m.

Some 7,000 pounds were used on April 19 to turn most of the building into twisted and hollowed-out carnage. The inanimate giant, which has – in a strange way – come to life over the past five weeks, survived the firing squad.

But today, it seemed to await a single officer who stepped forward, pulled a pistol, and put a bullet into its brain.

When the end came, it was swift, sure, and even surprising to those trained observers who had been glued to their vantage points since 5:30 a.m.

The Murrah Building was 18 when it died. Nearby at its death were downtown's older, more venerable, buildings like the Journal-Record Building and the Downtown YMCA, along with the Southwestern Bell Building and others.

Under a partly-cloudy sky and with a brisk wind blowing from the south, the explosive charges ignited. The warm spring air was filled with several short, loud reports, and the building was gone within the few seconds predicted by Controlled Demolitions International.

It seemed much quicker, but the operation was surgically precise and was carried out as planned. The center and elevator shift dropped forward to the north, then the east and west wings toppled inward.

A cloud of dust rose from the debris and was carried north to Seventh Street by the prevailing wind.

The sound seemed as fitting a memorial as Oklahoma City has witnessed yet. The several short, curt blasts came within nanoseconds of each other.

They formed a sound strangely similar to a 21-gun salute.

When the smoke had cleared five minutes later, the building had disappeared. It was like watching magician Doug Henning in a television act where he jerks a jetliner or the Statue of Liberty from your conscious view.

But this was no stunt, and the Murrah Building is no more.

I have thought about that day and that story many times over the decades. What I saw and felt standing on the Murrah Building Rubble will always be a part of me. The fact that all that carnage, death, and pain was inflicted upon so many innocents, and that it was the work of two right-wing extremists carrying a two-year-old grudge against the government, still seems insane.

As I've told the story of the bombing to my university students over the years, I rarely get through it without feeling a catch in my throat as the emotions swell up inside me. Each year, the date of April

19 reminds me of the horror that was unleashed in downtown Oklahoma City in 1995.

(This is a compilation of excerpts from stories I wrote for the Edmond Evening Sun when covering these events in 1995. Some of it appears in my book, The Long Pivot Home.)

The Willis Family of Oklahoma in the year 2000

20

The "Home" in Oklahoma

With my wanderlust always running at full speed in my younger years, I left my home state of Oklahoma in 1971 to see more of the country and find my adventures. I had lived nearly all my growing-up years here, and my town and state didn't seem to fit the bill of the special place I was seeing in my daydreams. I retained that mindset for many years as I moved from one part of America to another. Then I found myself back home again in the spring of 1995

Two American terrorists had just blown up the Alfred P. Murrah Federal building in Oklahoma City, a short drive from the front door of my childhood home in Midwest City. All of a sudden I started seeing this place differently. Before long, I had bonded anew with the city and state, and I've been writing about what happened there ever since.

Not all my writings have been in news stories or books. One day in the spring of 1998, I was driving back to Oklahoma to see my folks. I was living and working in Memphis at the time, and I'd forgotten how beautiful this state could be, especially when you're in its hills and trees. Driving past Lake Tenkiller, I started jotting down the names of these places and I put them together into a song. I called it, *The Home in Oklahoma*. It was my love song to my home state, and it can be heard in the playlist on my YouTube channel Windward319. Here are are the lyrics:

<u>The 'Home' in Oklahoma</u>

People pass through and ask,
"What's there to see?"
A native replies, "so much and it's free."
But when I come in from the east,
past the lakes and the trees,
I know the *home* in *Oklahoma*
was put there for me.

Sequoyah lived here,
taught his people to read;
Checotah, Okemah
let horses run free.
Tenkiller Dam lies beyond the next stream,
Yes the home in *Oklahoma*
is a place just for me.

Tahlequah's nestled

among these old hills,
Eufaula, Shawnee
beckon westwardly still;
This state's past is dusty
but now it's turned green,
Yes, the home in *Oklahoma*
was put there for me.
    I've traveled wide, I've moved far
to break free of this land,
There's got to be more,
I told my old friends;
But now the years have gone by
and clearly I see,
that the home in *Oklahoma*
was a clue meant for me.
    At a time when all Sooners
faced great misery,
Their hands came together,
their hearts bound by grief;
They showed the whole world
how to treat tragedy,
Yes, the home in *Oklahoma*
was put there just for me.
    The home in *Oklahoma*
is still waiting for me.
       ... 5/01/1998

Deciphering dreams are as hard as predicting chess moves.
TYC1989/Pixabay

21

Last Night I Had the Strangest Dream

"*Even a soul submerged in sleep is hard at work and helps make something of the world.*" -- Heraclitus.

Our dreamworld has been the subject of scientific scrutiny for a very long time. Like many other people, I've always wondered about my own dreams. Especially when they get wild and woolly, as can happen when illness dictates prescribed drugs that can affect those dreams. That happened this week, and it produced a doozy.

The med is *Benzonatate*, and my dosage is 100 mg. taken three times a day. Its side effect of hallucinatory dreams caught me off-guard last night, because I gave only a cursory glance at the label before downing the first pill.

Live and learn, although I'll stick with the prescription this week, because it does what it's supposed to do: it makes me cough *less*, thereby allowing me to absorb fewer punches to my rib cage when my current pneumonia hacking flares up.

I fell asleep quickly, but I was awakened about two hours later after a coughing spell zig-zagged past Big Ben and slammed hard against my ribs.

I looked across the bed at my slumbering wife and moved out to the couch recliner in the den so she could sleep in silence. It was 3 a.m., and I fell asleep almost immediately out there.

Then came The Dream:

It was late at night, and I had just arrived in a city that seemed familiar to me. I was with a group, and we had driven here to perform some vague public service job. The adrenaline was flowing as we unpacked our gear and settled into an inner-city hotel. Then we went to bed exhausted but were soon jarred awake by explosions and fires that lit up the streets outside.

Confusion, smoke and havoc were everywhere, and I lost track of the other group members who vanished in the chaos. I guessed everyone just scattered to help with whatever disaster was unfolding.

I was slow in getting started, as everything in the room was moving in slow motion. I groped around for my cell phone but could not find it. I reached around for my clothes and shoes, but no luck. Thankfully, I had worn my jeans to bed. Those were all I wore when I finally staggered outside alone and onto the crowded street.

Nothing seemed familiar, even though I felt I'd been in this city before. The explosion had changed everything. I had a general sense of which way to go, but I couldn't seem to make myself understood to others I passed when I asked for specific directions. Then there was this: I couldn't make my rubbery legs move right. So, I wobbled.

Out of nowhere, a kindhearted stranger appeared, saw me shivering in the night air, stopped, and gave me his coat. He wished me well, sat me down on a bench, then walked on.

I remember thinking I needed to call the editor at my newspaper to tell him I could cover this story, once I found out what the story really was. I considered it something important that I must do.

But I was feeling increasingly isolated from the crowd around me, I still didn't know where I was going or how to get there, and I began fading out, frustrated on many levels, yet oddly welcoming an encroaching restfulness.

Suddenly, I woke up and found myself standing right back in the middle of my den. All three of my dogs were sitting at my feet and staring straight up at me, expectantly.

It was 4 a.m., about an hour after I'd dozed off. I shook my head and looked around the darkened room.

"What the hell was *that* about?" I asked aloud to the dogs.

They didn't answer. Instead, hearing my voice, they relaxed, curled up and went back to sleep.

Then up pops these curious lyrics in my head from an old Kenny Rogers song called "The Kind of Fool Love Makes":

Anyone can read the signs,
or the writing on the wall;
It's all right there to see,
except someone like me,
who can't see the truth at all.

I decided to dissect what I'd just dreamed, what it was all about, and how I felt about it. I did this while knowing a smarter guy might say, just forget it. A dream is what it is, and it's probably nothing more than the trash heap of every weird thing that happened that day. Just move on. Get your sleep.

As my wife would tell you though, that's not me. I seldom meet a situation, idea, person -- or dream -- I don't want to analyze. Why should I change tonight?

Famed psychologist Carl Jung made a pretty good living doing his analyzing. He believed dreams come from our unconscious. He felt they reveal unique insights that can move us forward, get us unstuck, and help us grow. To him, dreams hold the wisdom of the unconscious mind, and they nudge us nightly toward a wider view of ourselves.

There is a catch, however. The mysterious *dream maker* lives in our unconscious mind and doesn't have a straight access to our consciousness. So, since it can't speak to us directly, it communicates in *symbol, image, metaphor, and emotion.* The dreamer must learn the *language* of the dream, and that skill doesn't come easy. The dreamer must decode those images and figure out why they seem important.

What matters is what the image means *to you.*

This dream was affecting me emotionally, so I set my doubts aside about Jung's method to give it a try.

Here's what I came up with:

The dream city was Oklahoma City, where I grew up and worked as a reporter before transitioning to college teaching. The havoc unleashed in the dream was the 1995 Oklahoma City bombing, and I was trying desperately to do what I actually *did* do in April of that year: report on the downtown bombing of the Alfred P. Murrah Federal Building and its human impact on Oklahoma.

The confusion displayed in the dream was what we *all* felt that day on April 19, and the desperation I personally felt was what I *really* did feel as I covered that attack. I wanted to provide answers to the legitimate questions everyone had. That took more than a month, but clearly the legacy of it is still a part of me, three decades later.

There were elements or images of the dream that didn't fit, however: I went into action partially naked, with little body control, and unable to interact with those around me before my senses faded out completely. What was all that about?

After all, I wasn't *killed* in the bombing. I was 15 miles away when it happened, and I didn't start reporting from Ground Zero until the next day. The only part that made *some* sense was not being fully clothed. By 1995, it had been years since I'd been reporting the news fulltime. Was I feeling *professionally* unclothed? Out of uniform? Did I still have the skills and instinct to do that job?

But why dream this dream *at all*, and what was my unconscious dream maker trying to tell me?

I developed two interpretations.

First, I was simply identifying with those 168 souls who died in the bombing and its aftermath. The clarity of feelings is nowhere better felt than in dreams. So, for the first time in 31 years, my subconscious took me into what dying might well have been like for these victims as they were losing the grip on their lives and losing contact with the living. Oddly, in my dream that didn't feel like an altogether horrific experience as the fade-out neared for me. A sense of peace was even present.

My second interpretation was that I was just feeling I was *ineffectual as a reporter* in helping readers understand fully what it was like in Oklahoma City that April 19, 1995. I tried hard to convey all of it, but words can only go so far.

I do know I grew as a journalist in covering this nightmare, and there were times I felt the "fire in my hands" that some writers are privileged to feel when their work has touched truth. But I don't know how well I translated that to the reader.

At the time, I took heart in knowing I broke through to at least *one* reader who mailed me a short note in the newsroom a few days after the smoke had cleared.

Unsigned, it read, *"Thank you, Sir. I lost a loved one in the bombing, and you made me feel like I was there. With her until the end."*

Whoever that person was, I've always regretted not being able to thank them. That's the best kind of compliment a writer can get.

So, sometime around 5 a.m. today, I thought about those two interpretations. I concluded they were *both* true. First -- because of a severe mid-life crisis, I was facing then, not connected to the bombing -- part of the old me *did* die with the Oklahoma City bombing. In covering that disaster, I found new strength to restart my own recovery as I wrote about the strength of these bombing survivors I interviewed.

And second, about the question of being ineffectual in my work, no ... I wasn't. But my effect was probably minimal. I tried, but I could have done a better job.

And, unlike dying, that's something I can live with.

Oh ... one other thing. The dude who gave me his coat that chilly night? I'm still working on that one.

I've got a good lead, though.

Feeling Whole Again in Oklahoma City

Oklahoma City April 19, 1998 -- I told myself I came back to visit my family, but I could have picked any weekend for that. For months in the back of my mind was this one weekend, especially Sunday, April 19. coming back to the bomb site three years later. Coming back to a pivotal point in my life. Coming back to remember ... and hopefully to feel again.

Five workmen are stopped in their tracks as they gaze across the street to the remains of the Murrah Federal building.
Jim Willis

Three years ago I had been revisiting my parents in Midwest City, taking a leave of absence from my teaching post at Boston College and trying to put the wheels back on my life's *Radio Flyer*. A shattering personal experience had left that child's wagon in pieces, scattered across a thousand miles of grieving.

I was searching for a way to forget. Or at least to deal with my pain. Then, on Wednesday morning, April 19, 1995, my personal pain collided with the far greater collective pain that emerged from the clouds of dust, debris, and devastation that was the bombing of the Alfred P. Murrah Federal Building.

Hearing a distant, undefinable sound from a diner in Norman, I didn't realize how this event would affect me personally. By the end of the day, that reality was streaming in like a door to a dark room opens slowly, allowing the outside light to seep in and gradually fill the room.

I have been in the news business for three decades and have seen many faces of tragedy during that time. There was the little girl who was killed by a falling beam as she sat in church one Sunday morning in Garland, Texas, 20 years ago. Then, ten years ago in Boston, Charles Stuart turned a gun on his pregnant wife, Carol, moments after emerging from a class on childbirth. Blaming it first on a black attacker, Stuart later took his own life after police realized he himself had been the shooter.

So many of these stories have occurred, and they tend to fade into a collective blur. But this story is different; this one will be remembered. This attack cost 168 innocent people their lives and injured some 800 others.

As a journalist who now teaches future reporters and editors, I have trained myself to put distance between me and the pain of others. I have coached my students to do the same. Remember what you are here for, I say. Do your job first. Remain detached. Yes, there are times when the pain invades you personally. But it is usually in the quiet, reflective moments after the tragedy, if in fact there is time for such moments. At some point in your life, that pain will come, whether you want it to or not.

Always, though, there are the exceptions. Thankfully, for me, Oklahoma City was that exception in the spring of 1995. It may sound macabre to say I found a renewed energy and life force in this tragedy.

But I did. I found it in joining with others who were grieving over something much more painful. What a privilege it was to have the chance to articulate their pain. What a catharsis it was to be able to release my own in the process.

I will always be grateful to the Edmond Evening Sun, the newspaper where I began my career many years ago, for putting me at the bomb site and allowing me to report on its aftermath.

Over the three years since the bombing, I have spoken to many groups, both in the United States and Europe, about covering this tragedy in Oklahoma City. Always the thought is within me that I grew personally and moved beyond my personal grief as I watched survivors and families of the victims do the same.

In telling their story of survival, I was also telling my own. To myself, anyway.

On a professional level, I had been confronting burnout with this business of journalism going into April 19, 1995. I wondered if there was any real purpose in exposing other's pain, problems, and perils.

By the end of my first day of bombing coverage, I found a new meaning to this profession. I am sure the same has happened to reporters covering other such tragedies.

Such journalism puts all humanity on the same page in the hymnal of brotherhood and sisterhood, understanding and support. Such journalism is washed clean of the manipulation and sensationalism of pseudo-news and trash reporting. Such journalism deals openly with the gut questions that friends and families of the dead and suffering are desperately seeking answers to. *What happened? Who did it? Why? Who died? Am I safe now? What can I learn from it?*

Some of these deeper questions lie beyond the purview of journalism, which is basically, history on the run. The larger answers are found in discussions with loved ones, or in reading the thoughts of those wonderful writers gifted at thoughtful reflection. Or the answers may surface in spiritual counseling.

But journalism can help. It can open the doors to the mind and heart as it shows all of us that we are not alone in our grief and there are others who can help us.

And it can make even the most objective of us feel the emotions that make us real people.

Sunday night, with all ten fingers laced through the chain-link fence separating the mourners from the insanity of that bombing, with my eyes fixed on the hallowed ground before me, and with the vivid memory of what that killing ground looked like three years ago, the feelings returned.

I knew that in feeling for others and helping to articulate their pain, I was becoming whole again.

Germany, the country that overcame the next-door threat of communism, is where I go to get my freedom batteries recharged.

Analogicus/Pixabay

23

When Your World Expands, Embrace It

While I love to talk about my times in Oklahoma, the place that finishes close behind it is actually a *country*. Its people call it

Deutschland, we call it Germany but, either way, the Germans I've known are some of the finest people in the world.

Before 1995, I had never been to Germany. Since 1995, I've made more than 20 trips there, each time as a journalist or a lecturer (sometimes both), but always for enjoyment and enlightenment. You get an added perspective on the world when you travel to Europe, and it's always a learning experience.

In the process, I've made several wonderful friends and have had opportunities to bring many of them back to the states to further their own understanding of how professional journalists apply their craft here.

Despite policy differences, mostly centering on America's involvement in conflicts and wars around the world, most Germans have long considered America to be their staunchest international ally. Their American heroes are John F. Kennedy, and they also loved Barack Obama as president. On the GOP side, they appreciated the work Ronald Reagan and George Bush Sr. did in bringing down the Berlin Wall and ending Communism in Europe, along with the help of former Russian premier Mikhail Gorbachev.

That's why it is sad to see the German/American alliance fall on hard times under President Donald Trump, whose America First agenda doesn't resonate well in Germany or most of the rest of Europe. His suggestions that America may leave the NATO Alliance don't help matters, and our standing in the eyes of the world has dropped. It's important to note that, since the end of World War II, Germany has rebuilt itself into everything the Nazis were *not*. To that end, this country has become the most pacifistic of world nations over the decades. Until recently, under pressure from NATO, they had never put their troops into any foreign conflicts.

The German dimension of my life began in the fall of 1995, just after I had joined the Journalism faculty at the University of Memphis. I held an endowed chair position which kept my class load small and allowed me time to travel for research and lecturing purposes. One day

I received a letter from the American Embassy, then in Bonn, inviting me to conduct a lecture tour at several universities across Germany.

The invitation came from Dr. Martina Kohl, public affairs specialist for the embassy. It would be the first of many lecture tours I would make for the U.S. State Department and its Foreign Service. Martina and I became very good friends over the years and still stay in touch today. I admire her and her success in furthering the German/America bond.

This invitation was part of the public diplomacy efforts of what was then the United States Information Service (called the USIA in America). Their main goal was to assist international understanding, and the program they set up for that was the Amerika Haus program.

At the time, the U.S. State Department was officially separated from Amerika Haus in order to take politics out of what was deemed to be an objective effort at explaining America to Germans. Amerika Haus Libraries were set up in several locations throughout Germany and Europe. They were street-front operations where Europeans could walk in and learn about the U.S. Many students used these libraries to get information on American colleges, and many applied for student visas to do a year or more of college studies in the states.

I was asked to come and talk about a book I had just written called, *The Age of Multimedia and Turbonews*. But they also wanted to hear about my coverage of the Oklahoma City bombing and other major news stories. The O.J. Simpson trial was one of them.

Within a month, I was welcomed in Frankfurt and began the tour that would take me to universities in Nuremberg, Giessen, Mainz, Dresden (formerly behind the Iron Curtain in East Germany.)

It was a fascinating tour, and I learned a lot about Germans in the process. I came to develop a fond affection for them and their country.

Two of the first things I learned were that they obey the laws of their cities and country to the letter, and they do the same in conserving energy, and in preferring specific statements to ambiguous ones.

Examples? Try these:

On my first day in Giessen, I was walking near the university and crossed the street at an intersection. When I got to the other side, a woman stopped me and said politely yet sternly, "You broke the law there, young man. You needed to wait for the crosswalk light to turn green." Then she bid me a good day.

The next day I was working late in a university office, was tired and left the building without turning my office lights off. The next morning, the department chair called me into his office and said, "Jim, you probably didn't know this, but in Germany, we always turn the lights off when we leave. However, we seldom have the lights on, because it is our custom that we finish our work before it turns dark so we can save electricity from those lights."

Later that day, the same faculty member asked when I'd like to go to dinner that evening. "Oh, how about around 6?" I said. He looked puzzled and then said, "So is that 5:45 or 6:15?" Actually, I appreciated this German trait because I'm a stickler for on-time meetings and arrivals myself.

Even though those may not have been universal German traits, ever since then I've never left the lights on when I leave a room there, I always wait for the crosswalk lights to turn green, and I am always specific about meet-up times!

This first of many ensuing lecture trips turned out to be the most important for me, because it was there I met a giant of a man named Fritz Hattig. I was asked to talk with journalists at ZDF Television, headquartered in Mainz, one afternoon and there was Fritz at the front of the reception line to greet me.

Dr. Fritz Hattig, my friend.

Fritz was a Renaissance man. He was in his 60s and serving as director of educational and social policies at the TV network. In his younger years he had been an Olympic-level athlete, playing field handball for both the German and (by special arrangement) the U.S. National Teams. He became well known in Germany for his own athletic prowess and then as one of the main sports journalists in the country for German Television ZDF.

He went on to get a Ph.D. and was tapped by Willi Daume, president of the 1972 Munich Olympics to be his top assistant in running those games.

If you remember your history, these games were overshadowed by the eight Palestinian terrorists of the Black September terrorist group who killed two Israeli athletes, took nine other athletes from the team hostage, then killed all of them at the Munich Airport when a West German rescue mission failed on the runway. Five of the eight terrorists were killed by West German security forces, but a German police officer was also killed.

The surviving three Palestinians were arrested and jailed, but were freed in an international hostage exchange a month later when a Lufthansa passenger plane was hijacked by Palestinians. The Israeli government sent the Mossad on an assassination mission to track down and kill anyone who played a role in the massacre in Munich.

Fritz blamed himself, in part, for the terrorists' ability to infiltrate the Olympic Village where the athletes were abducted. He was a member of the German organizing committee of the Olympics that decided *not* to arm the guards in the village.

"We wanted to show the world that the new Germany was a non-violent country and put to rest our past Nazi image," Fritz told me. "This was nearly 30 years after World War II ended, and we felt it was time for that worldview of us to die. So, we didn't arm our security guards."

Fritz himself was one of the most non-violent men I've ever known. He was deeply influenced by his childhood when he grew up in Berlin while the city was being bombed into rubble toward the end of WWII. When the war ended, he credited the Marshall Plan of extending Allied help to Germany to rebuild. It was that plan that made him come to love America instead of hating it.

On a personal level, here's how it played out for Fritz as an 11-year-old child and how that terrible beginning carried over into a fine manhood.

"I was out in the streets of Berlin trying to do what I could to find food for my mother, brothers and sisters," he told me. He was the oldest of the eight siblings. "One day, when American troops were still in the city, I was picking up rubble for a little money for groceries. An American soldier came up and gave me two chocolate candy bars. I was so hungry. He shook my hand and then went on his way. I will never forget that. I was a proud German, but that soldier's kindness was what made me want to be an American."

After graduating from college in Germany and then getting his Ph.D. at the University of Hanover, he did go to America and took a visiting faculty position at Southern Illinois University in Carbondale. Then came his chance to pay America back for the Marshall Plan and those candy bars the American G.I. gave him in Berlin.

He accepted a position teaching German at the United States Military Language School in Monterey, California.

So, decades later, Fritz and I met. We took a liking to each other immediately, and we hatched a plan to secure one of his personal goals at ZDF Television.

"I want our journalists, especially those who cover America, to perfect their English and to really understand how you journalists do things in America," he said. "Can you help me do that, Jim?"

We set up and implemented an international study tour, at least once a year, to send groups of ZDF news employees to the University of Memphis where I was teaching. There, I would organize a week's worth of sessions with the group and discuss how America works at the grassroots level and how journalists do their work. I would bring in working journalists and also set up parts of the day where ZDF employees could go to local news stations and shadow the news crews on their reporting assignments.

These trips became a reality the next year, with several more such training sessions following them. But, as the first one began, I saw that what Fritz wanted most for these staffers was for them to learn to speak English the way Americans spoke it, complete with as many of our sayings and colloquialisms as possible.

Often, Fritz would stop me as I or others spoke when he heard a term or phrase he wanted his fellow ZDF'ers to learn. For example, once I described on-air news talent as needing to be "easy on the eyes," something Fritz had never heard. So I explained it to the group. Another time, my wife Anne used the phrase, "wall-to-wall news coverage" and, again, Fritz paused the session as Anne compared it to "wall-to-wall carpets," something they could understand.

True to his German nature, Fritz was always very direct when he said things, and didn't mince words in telling his staff members to "pay attention to this!" He was also a born organizer, and overdid it as a micro-manager of his group. So much so that his co-workers began calling him "the Pope."

I've never had so much fun getting to know people as I did these Germans from ZDF. They were such talented, determined, yet very gentle people. Often I would have them over to my home for dinner, and I remember one night in particular when I was nearly reduced to tears.

I was playing some background music on my CD player, and a Karen Carpenter tune came on. The player was back in my bedroom, and I noticed one of the ZDF staffers wandered back in there to hear it better. His name was Abi, and I followed him to the room.

When I entered, Abi was standing over the CD player and he was weeping.

"Abi," I asked, "What's wrong? Are you feeling bad?"

He looked up slowly, wiping away tears. "I'm sorry, Jim, but I loved Karen Carpenter, and I still can't believe she died so young! Every time I hear her voice, I cry for her and for what happened to her."

I put my arm over his shoulder and told him I get that urge myself. Then the moment passed, and we went back to join the group in the living room.

Two other moments stand out as well for me during that ZDF visit in Memphis. Fritz wanted to make sure his staff came into contact with as many aspects of Americana as possible. So I took them to places like Elvis' home Graceland, the Civil War battlefield Shiloh, about 90 minutes east of Memphis, and a concert by the Beach Boys.

I think it was that concert where I really saw these Germans cut loose and enjoy themselves. The Beach Boys are American as it gets, and the ZDF crew was there to see America. Before the night was over, these dozen Germans abandoned their cultural stoicism and were dancing in the aisle to *Help Me Rhonda*, as Fritz leading the charge with a huge smile adorning his face. If the goal was to get Fritz and his crew experiencing Americana, and doing it with glee, then mission accomplished.

And I was feeling very good. I will always remember Fritz that way.

There would be many other meetings with Fritz, both in Germany and in Memphis, and he always seemed so happy to see me, and so upset when my schedule in Germany didn't allow me to go to Mainz and see him. Usually, the next time that I could see him, he would start in by haranguing for "not taking the time to even see me on your last trip!" But the next second he would throwing his arms around me in a bear hug, laugh, and let me off the hook for my previous faux pas.

But a few years later, after I left Memphis and was teaching at Ashland University in Ohio in 2006, I saw that the sad Fritz – the one who remembered the Munich Olympics – was still unable to shake that memory. It happened when I invited him to come and speak to our students about those Olympics when the film *Munich,* was playing across America. This is the movie that focused on the Mossad's assassinations of surviving culprits involved in the Munich Massacre.

Fritz seemed excited about it, and we were glad to have him. But he also seemed nervous, so I decided to have a different format for his presentation. Instead of just putting him up alone in front of an auditorium of students, I asked him if he would prefer we do a Q&A format with me – and afterward the students – ask him specific questions about Munich. He thanked me for this plan and said yes, it would be better.

When the evening arrived for his presentation, I knew this was the right format. His unease disappeared as he responded to my questions and then interacted with the students. I realized I had never heard Fritz deliver a speech before and I sensed this was not the time to experiment and hope for the best. Fritz was always so exuberant that he often got off track, and I didn't want him to come all the way to America just to be embarrassed by doing it in front of a couple hundred students.

The evening went splendidly, and Fritz was able to return to Germany with a happy and proud memory of doing so well in the America he still loved passionately.

For his work in furthering international relations between Germany and America, Fritz was honored in 1994 and again in 2001. That second celebration was held at the Consular General residence in Frankfurt, where both Fritz and I were given certificates of achievement for our work in developing and implementing the professional American Studies programs in Memphis for ZDF staffers.

Sadly, Fritz Hattig passed away in 2016. He was a good friend, and I miss him.

24

Germans Celebrate 25 Years of Freedom

Euphoria at the Wall just after it was breached by the East German people in November, 1989.

Pixabay

BERLIN -- When 23-year-old Klaus Schroter was making his fatal run across the death strip to scale the Berlin Wall in 1964, he could only dream about a scene like the one at the foot of the Brandenburg Gate tonight.

He and 135 known others were gunned down trying to reach freedom during the 28 years the Berlin Wall stood, and tonight thousands of Berliners honored them for their heroism.

The 25th anniversary of the Mauerfall, as the Germans call the fall of the Wall, was spectacular and awe-inspiring. While the main event was supposed to be the timed release of nearly 8,000 LED-illuminated balloons into the night sky, the show at the foot of Germany's national monument stole the spotlight and had the crowd applauding and even cheering.

That is saying something for a people not generally known for overt displays of emotion. But then, this was their party and the spotlight was on them as the prime agents who brought down the wall 25 years ago tonight.

"The government leaders would come along and take credit for it later, but it was the ordinary people who tore down the Berlin Wall," said Stefan Domelt, a communications consultant who was one of the many who came to celebrate the anniversary. "The people were the ones who showed up at the border crossings and demanded to pass that night; not the politicians."

The story has been told many times of this great accident in German history, when a confused East German border guard (Col. Harald Jaeger) couldn't make sense of ambiguous orders and let a stream of East Germans pass to West Berlin. The stream became a river and then an ocean of freedom-loving eastern Europeans who had been denied their liberties for 28 years.

Within a year, East and West Germany would be reunified officially into one Germany.

So, just as they did in 1999 and again in 2009, Germans from all over the country came to this capital city to celebrate. The main difference between this event and the 20th anniversary was the focus on the ordinary German people and not on the government leaders who had been so prominently featured in 2009.

Not to be totally left out, however, both Russia's Mikhail Gorbachev, now 83, and Poland's Lech Walesa, 71, were featured briefly on stage with other dignitaries. But they did not speak and were part of what amounted to more of a quick parade so the attention could be turned back to the German people.

Those who did speak, did so between rousing live concerts by German pop star Clusoe, the band Silly, and a scheduled performance by American Peter Gabriel. The speakers were not politicians, but were citizen leaders of the East German protest movement. And often during the performances, images on the six large screens would shift to the crowd in the plaza who had come to celebrate.

A multimedia show featured videos of the night of Nov. 9, 1989, when East Germans poured through the various border crossings and had an all-night party in West Berlin.

But the most poignant moment of a night filled with earth-shaking music and perfected light and laser shows, was when a lone drummer stepped onstage, to be joined by another. As they started their beat, the screen lit up with panels of black and white pictures of the 136 known East Germans who were killed trying to scale the Berlin Wall between 1961 and 1989.

The crowd was silent at first, then broke into spontaneous applause and cheers for their fallen citizens whose only crime was to make a run for freedom.

That was followed by a huge choir singing, "Die Gedanken Sind Frei," meaning, "Ideas are free." Then came a giant slide of a famed panel from the East Side Gallery, where a mile-long stretch of the remaining wall serves as concrete canvas for artists. It underscored the role of the people in bringing down the wall

and read, "Many small people, in many small places, do many small things that can alter the face of the world."

Once again, the throng broke into applause.

This anniversary was a big deal in German. Television stations had been going wall-to-wall with live coverage of performances and events from Brandenburg Gate all day.

Despite the festivities, some Germans believe all these anniversaries and constant comparisons of East and West Germans are annoying and should end; others believe the fall of the Wall was so important that it should be remembered and cherished. These ceremonies help do that, they say.

Steffen Dobbert, 32, who was a young child in East Germany said of the celebrations, "They are as superfluous as a goiter." He told the

Hamburger Time that he doesn't feel, think, or act any differently than western Germans.

But Anne Hahnig, 26, born in Freiberg, says differences show up soon in conversations between easterners and westerners. She believes in what she calls the "three-minute rule."

"After three minutes of conversation, the differences would appear. Because East Germans earn less, and fathers take 'parental leave' to find work in the West."

On my first lecture trip to Germany in November, 1995, I was speaking at the University of Dresden in the former East Germany. This was only six years after the fall of the Wall, and Russian was still the main second language of that area. So I needed a translator in my lecture hall, as many college students were still trying to replace Russian with English. After my lecture, a group of Dresden students accompanied me to a local biergarten where we had a chance to talk more personally. This group seemed to be more familiar with English, so the conversation went late into the night.

They spoke of being in their early teens when the Wall came down in November, 1989, and of how joyous that evening was. They had taken a train to Berlin just to be a part of the celebration. But then they said something that I found especially interesting.

"Although it was wonderful on the night of November 9," a student named Gunther said, "the next morning was a little different story. The world we awoke to had all changed for us. We knew we were on the road to being much more a free people, and that Soviet Communism was on the way out. But with it, went a lot of economic security for us. Under Communism, we did suffer oppression by the State, but that state also took care of our basic needs. We had a place to live and enough food to live on. Most people were assured of work.

"But, all of a sudden, we knew we were going to have to go look for our own jobs as we entered a capitalist economy, and jobs could be hard to find. Money for food was not a guarantee any more, and we were going to have to look out for ourselves. Most of us still welcomed the new system when we rejoined West Germany, but we also knew it would not be easy."

Dr. Thomas Nenon, a University of Memphis dean who graduated from Germany's Freiburg University and spends much time there, calls the fall of the Wall, "the most significant event in German consciousness perhaps since World War II."

Opinions about reunification remain mixed, however. An October poll shows Germans still describe each other's character based on their regional origin (east or west). In that poll, 50 percent of all Germans polled described themselves as "winners" as a result of reunification. Some 23 percent said they saw themselves as "losers," while 27 percent did not respond to the question.

The top three reasons why easterners say that there is a reason to feel like a winner are freedom to travel, freedom of speech, and free elections.

These results are consistent with comments made Friday by three staff members of the American Embassy in Berlin.

Cornelia Voss was a librarian who lived for three decades in East Berlin. When the Wall came down, she was bewildered by what would come next. There was anticipation, but also angst.

"I knew right away I'd lost my job," she said Friday. "So many of us where thrown out of work. Our
system changed right away."

Those changes meant uncertainty, and not all the changes were helpful ones for former East Germans.

"I was confused about the new laws and regulations of West Germany," she said.

"It was good for me, though, that it happened early in my career," she said. "Older workers had even more trouble getting new jobs."

Still, Voss was unemployed for a year until she found new work in the West. An East German university degree in library science didn't count for much in the new Germany, she said.

25 Years past the fall of the Wall, 2014
Jim Willis

But Germans like Voss are used to learning how to survive and succeed. For many years now, she has been on the staff of the American Embassy in Berlin. Ironically, she now is responsible for handling public correspondence and deals with concerns and complaints Germans have about American policies and actions.

So how do former East Germans feel about the Mauerfall 25 years later?

"It's who you ask and how old they are," Voss said. "Younger people are more positive about reunification; older people may not be."

A colleague of Voss, Geertje Huendorf, was also raised in the former GDR (German Democratic Republic, or East Germany). But Huendorf was only 14 when the wall fell. That made her experience different from Voss'.

"I was part of the lucky generation," she said. "That's what we call ourselves, because our opportunities were better since the world opened up to us when the wall came down at a young age. I was able to go to the U.S. as an exchange student."

Her continued educational experience, plus her intimate knowledge of living under a Communist system, made Huendorf very marketable. Today she is a public affairs specialist for International Security Issues with the American Embassy in Berlin.

Huendorf noted that there were certain "basic needs" taken care of for people in the GDR, and that older Germans from the East remember that when economic times get tough for them now. That is a key reason why – still today – polls reveal not all former East Germans are happy about reunification with the West.

When the Wall fell and reunification followed later in the year, the Communist economy was replaced by free market capitalism. With it, came new currency and higher prices. Also East Germans, who had depended on the GDR meeting basic needs, were thrust into an open job market that couldn't really accommodate everyone. That flood of new job-seekers was seen as a threat by many West Germans.

Dr. Martina Kohl, longtime cultural affairs specialist with the American Embassy in Berlin put it this way:

"Some communities are doing well in the East, but some aren't. Potsdam and Leipzig are doing well, but others struggle. Some western regions are hurting, too, though. It's a mixed bag. Some eastern regions are losing their young people to the West, and that hurts them."

"The key is the local mayors," Kohl said. "What are they doing to keep young people interested in staying in their regions? The mayors make a big, big difference, and some of them are succeeding with programs designed to keep young people in the region."

(Portions of this are excerpted from my story I wrote for The Oklahoman in covering the 25th anniversary of the "Mauerfall" in November, 2014)

25

Immigrants, Germany and Luther

Lutherstadt Wittenberg and Berlin, Germany – As a young man, Martin Luther had a persistent, obsessive fear that he was a refugee, cast out from God's grace, and that it was his own fault.

"My sin lay heavy night and day," he wrote. Later, he would lament, "To be convinced in our hearts that we have forgiveness of sins and peace with God by grace alone is the hardest thing."

Then, after nailing his 95 Theses to the door of All Saints Church in Wittenberg on Oct. 31, 1517, Luther risked becoming

A large wall mural in Wittenberg depicts Luther's hand in the Bible.
Jim Willis

a refugee from his homeland as well. Leaders in the Roman Catholic Church were aiming their arrows of persecution squarely at him.

Today, 500 years later in Germany, many who visit the exhibits of the Reformation 2017 anniversary find a Luther who is easier to identify with than they had ever imagined. And they are pondering what his Reformation should mean for them personally and for their society today.

It would be incorrect to overstate the influence of this Reformation 2017 celebration on Germans' feelings about refugees, it would also be wrong to understate it. Millions of Germans feel attached to Luther, and, to them, he is urging them to welcome those refugees.

"Luther was so human," said Dr. Markus Ziener, a veteran journalist with the influential German newspaper Handelsblatt who now heads a university journalism department in Berlin. "Because he struggled, the rest of us who struggle can identify with him and find him very approachable," Ziener said.

Judging himself an undeserving sinner, Luther had set out on a personal quest to discover how he might access the grace of God and be a refugee no more.

That quest led him to study theology, the Bible, and the writings of Augustine, and that is where he met a different, merciful Christ. He couldn't wait to tell others about how they could find this man of mercy, too.

So, when Luther sat down to write his 95 theses in 1517, *he was driven by a few simple, democratic ideas: that the grace of God is available to every believer and that everyone is equally free to access that grace on their own. Armed with that knowledge, Christians were then to help others in need.*

The rest is history.

Somehow, though, over the years immediately following Luther and through the centuries beyond, that simple message of equality and openness has gotten muddled. The 500-year-old tree that has grown from Luther's roots has taken on a lot of branches, some of which are gnarled and appear to belong to another tree entirely. Luther's vision of unity instead became divisiveness among Christians. His vision of peace instead became the Thirty Years War. And, in the 20th century, his vision was co-opted by Adolph Hitler to justify the rise and practices of the Third Reich, as both Protestant and Catholic leaders in Germany bought into that thinking, at least for a time.

"God does not need your good works, but your neighbor does." (Luther)

Happily, other branches of the Luther tree look like they are exactly where they belong. You could call one of them the branch of openness, and that one is blossoming in Germany today as the country celebrates one of its truest heroes.

How much do Germans revere Martin Luther? A national survey taken a few years ago by a public television station asked viewers to rate the most influential Germans of all time. Luther finished second, behind post-war Chancellor Konrad Adenauer, according to Dr. H.C. Volker Faigle, former chaplain to the German Parliament.

You hear a lot of Germans talking about Luther and about openness these days, as the country has welcomed 1.4 million refugees since 2015. That was the year that some one million of those immigrants, mostly from the Middle East, entered Germany. Since then, the numbers have dropped to about 200,000 a year because of Turkey's tightening of its borders. But with the 500th anniversary of the Reformation being celebrated here, many Germans are interpreting Luther's visions a call to continue offering safe haven to those refugees running for their lives.

This is happening in a country where 67 percent of Germans profess Christianity, with the Protestant Evangelical Church and the Roman Catholic Church having roughly equal membership.

So, after centuries of some twisted interpretations of Luther came and went, this particular meaning of inclusion finally seems to parallel what the Wittenberg monk had in mind when he began writing back in the 16th century. That meaning is found in the gospel of Matthew:

"I was a stranger, and you invited me in." (Matthew 25:35)

That verse is a driver for Germans like Dr. Faigle, a Berliner on a mission with a speed to his step and a tireless energy that defies his autumnal years. He gets very animated when he thinks of Matthew 25. He believes it is an essential lesson that Martin Luther wanted us all to learn, and he believes it has great relevance to the immigration issue that Germany and other countries are facing.

Faigle knows something about the intersection of faith and politics in Germany. The ordained Lutheran minister has served as ambassador of the EKD (the 23 million-member Protestant Evangelical Church of Germany) to both Germany and the European Union, served as chaplain to the Parliament, and counts leaders like Chancellor Angela Merkel and South African Bishop Desmond Tutu as his friends. In Berlin, Faigle just completed a three-year stint heading the church council of the Berliner Dom – commonly called The Cathedral – a historic Lutheran church that welcomes 1,500 daily visitors and is Berlin's largest Protestant church.

"Luther is very present in Germany today," Faigle said in an interview at the Hotel Albrechtshof, that also serves as a stadtmission, or city mission. "He was the father of our democracy. He believed each of us to be a free person, subject only to the will of God, and that this is offered to everyone. And because of this, you will

serve others."

"Dialogue. Dispute. Renewal. We were born for mutual conversation." (Phillip Melanchton, collaborator of Luther.)

Faigle believes serving others means welcoming immigrants into Germany, especially those fleeing danger. He is not alone in that thinking, and he pointed to recent surveys to support his belief that others are connecting Luther's teachings with Germans' desire to help the refugees.

A refugee family awaits its time to start processing to stay in Germany.

Jim Willis

"That [connection] is very present," he said. "In a recent national survey, three out of four Germans said yes, I'm ready to help with the immigrants. And one out of 10 is actively involved in helping them."

He also sees the spirit of Luther in Chancellor Merkel as she has become "Mama Merkel" to the many new refugees she has let into Germany.

"Here you can now see her Christian background," Faigle asserted. "She said, 'These people suffer, and we are a free society. We are going to help.'" He continued,

"The dignity of the human being is sacred. If a person is facing persecution, then the German thinking is we have to take them in."

Faigle explained that standard visa requirements "went out the window" as Merkel opened the doors wide. So, technically, "What she did was totally illegal," he said. "But our church begged her to do it from the beginning."

Faigle, who knows many in Parliament personally because of his time as chaplain, says most of its members are driven by Christian values and agree with Merkel that granting asylum is the humanitarian thing to do.

Although separation of church and state is a guiding policy in Germany, the government is also helping to fund Reformation 2017, seeing it as a major cultural event but also, according to Faigle, because the government sees value in people practicing their religion. Lawmakers also authorized the release of a special commemorative Martin Luther briefmarke or stamp in honor of the Reformation's anniversary.

"The majority of those in Parliament are driven by Christian values, and the government says yes we need religious values," he said. "We want people to exercise religion as long as it is in line with the free democratic principles of Germany. But everyone has a right to believe whatever they believe."

"Against each other, side by side, together." (Reformation 2017 banner)

Faigle believes the coverage by German media are helping remind people of Christian values and responsibilities by focusing so much attention on the anniversary that Germans often call "Luther 500."

"Many stories are about what role Luther played in our German society. He is the father of German democracy! Even the German Parliament passed a resolution eight or ten years ago that said the Reformation has had worldwide impact."

David Rising, chief correspondent for the Associated Press in Berlin, confirmed that the Reformation story is a big one for German media and that most Germans are aware of the anniversary celebrations. He also noted that the immigration debate in Germany, which reached a fever pitch in 2015, has greatly abated as the numbers of immigrants have dropped to 200,000 annually.

This doesn't mean Germans are not still divided, however, over perceived dangers of granting asylum to refugees from the Middle East. Following the massive influx of refugees in 2015, just over half of the German population responding to a 2016 ZDF Television poll expressed doubts that the country could successfully handle such an influx. Still, some 57 percent said they didn't think putting an upper limit on immigration would work either.

Undeterred, Faigle noted that Luther himself wrote a treatise in 1517 promoting the duty of churches to offer asylum to refugees. He said he knows of 45 refugees marked for deportation have found sanctuary in German churches.

But an official with the Save the Children organization in Berlin says that the number of refugees receiving asylum is much higher. Save the Children has seen an integral leader in helping refugee children find safe spaces after they arrive in the new country.

"The churches also play a role when it comes to helping in cases of imminent deportations of refugees because they are allowed to give them church asylum," said Desiree Weber, project manager for the STS Children on the Move program. "We know of 321 cases of church asylum with all in all 539 people. 261 of the cases are so called Dublin cases (an EU law allowing states to return refugees to the state through which the refugee first entered the EU.)"

In that vein, the Berliner Dom is heavily involved in helping refugees in Berlin, and the memory of Luther's mandate is one of their drivers. The Cathedral went so far as to set up cubicle housing, right on their grounds, for upwards to 45 refugees. After being advised by the government that providing enough security for those refugees there was impossible, the church shifted an equivalent amount of funding to other, more secure refugee centers.

"Reformation means shaping the future." (Reformation 2017 slogan)

Underscoring the Reformation/refugee connection is Professor Gerhard Robbers, chairman of the steering committee of Reformation 2017, the celebration that is reaching its peak this summer in Wittenberg, a half-hour train ride from Berlin and the home of Martin Luther. It is a town that has mixed history with fun for young and old alike. Here you find everything from somber seminars on what the Reformation means for today's Germany, mixed with festivities complete with concerts, balloons bounce houses, and magic shows for kids.

"Refugees are a main topic throughout the Reformation anniversary events, "Robbers said. "We are organizing several events ... In all of these events, the topic of refugees will be of key interest. For example, during the time of the Weltausstellung Reformation (World Exhibition on the Reformation) there is a daily discussion forum on refugees. The Wittenberg exhibition is structured by thematic weeks such as Justice, Human Rights, One World, Peace, etc. Refugees are of central importance in any of those."

The Wittenberg exhibition, which is spread around and across this entire 1,000-year-old town of 50,000 people where Luther preached and nailed his 95 Theses to the doors of All Saints Church, began on May 20 and runs to Sept. 10. On its opening weekend, it drew more than 100,000 visitors to town, highlighting one of the most visible connections of the Reformation and refugees is in Wittenberg, Robbers noted. "There are seven Gates of Freedom a within the city - one of which is dedicated to refugees depicting abstract replicas original refugee boats on the lake.

Also, on the Deutsche Evangelische Kirchentag (German Protestant Church Day) in Berlin one of the main thematic areas is refugees."

Robbers was speaking of Gate 4 in Wittenberg, labeled the Gate of Justice, Peace, and Integrity of Creation. Here, visitors could stroll around the Swan Pond where the wooden frames of several boats – meant to represent the flimsy craft the refugees are taking from countries like Syria – float on the water in various states of disrepair. The sign-guided tour invites visitors to reflect on a world full of injustice and violence and asks what our response should be.

Meanwhile, at Gate 5 for Globalization and One-World Unity, the architectural metaphor is the "Church of Light," an A-framed chapel made of translucent material allowing light in and out as worshippers meditate within.

Overseeing that exhibit is Rudolf Wenz, a Wittenberg psychotherapist who counsels a different kind of outcast: drug and alcohol addicts as they go through detox and recovery. When asked his thoughts on Germany's refugee crisis, his response was immediate.

"What crisis? Why is it a crisis?" asked this big, wry man, serious about his mission but also with a dash of humor to his voice. "The only crisis is the old people need to get out of the way and let the young people come in. We need them. Germany has always been a country of outsiders. After the War, we brought in – what – four million refugees. No one said that was too many too soon."

Asked why he became a volunteer for Reformation Summer, he said his church (a congregation of the EKD) is sponsoring the exhibit and he felt it was important to help.

"Our Church of Light symbolizes the light of Christ and His openness to all," Wenz said, adding that is a key theme of the Globalization Gate. "Christ said, 'Come unto me.' He did not discriminate. So our church is a place to sit and meditate, or simply to come in out of the rain."

Then that humor, coupled with a sigh, revealed itself again: "But it's our talking robot that seems to get more attention."

(This is an excerpt of a longer story I originally wrote for Christianity Today Magazine in 2017, at a time when America was -- and still is -- looking for answers to its own immigration issues.)

26

Me, I've Lived in Dreams

I've done a lot of dreaming, often while playing the guitar, over the years. All that work paid off in the year 2000.

With apologies to Judy Collins for the line that makes up this title, I have spent a lot of time in my life dreaming. Specifically, dreaming about love and when it might come my way. In my dreams, I have discovered I can feel pure, unfiltered emotions in ways that I usually can't in my waking hours. Now, those emotions can indeed range from fear, to anger, and to pride, but the one I often feel clearest is love.

I love to dream, and I love listening to music. So it's not surprising that I like songs about dreaming. They have helped keep hope alive over the years.

Judging by the long list of songs that tie together dreams with love, it appears I'm definitely not alone when I dream about love.

Here are a few of the tunes over the decades that have boosted the belief of so many music lovers that love is within our grasp.

All you gotta' do is dream, right?

Every night, I hope and pray, a dream lover will come my way; a girl to hold in my arms, and know the magic of her charms.

I can still hear Bobby Darin and Rick Nelson each crooning **Dream Lover** on the radio back in 1959, and it would be soon be a go-to song whenever my love life was looking grim.

When I feel blue in the night, I need you to hold me tight; Whenever I want you, all I have to do is dream.

The Everly Brothers had a big-time hit when **All I Have to Do is Dream** came out in 1958, and it validated my fantasy notion that this would be how I would find my love.

Dream until your dreams come true.

Steven Tyler and Aerosmith found fame with **Dream On** in 1973, reiterating the same tip from the Everly Brothers 15 years earlier.

Dream baby, got me dreamin' sweet dreams, the whole day through.

In 1962, Roy Orbison released his blockbuster of **Dream, Dream, Baby,** just as my high school dating life was starting to pick up steam. And, to me, that was one steamy song.

You gotta follow that dream wherever that dream may take you, you gotta follow that dream wherever it may lead.

From the 1962 movie of the same name, **Follow That Dream** is a fast-paced tune was belted out by The King himself, Elvis. I figured if there's one guy in the world who knows something about getting girls, it's gotta be him. So I followed my dream.

In dreams I walk with you, in dreams I talk with you. In dreams you're mine, all of the time.

In 1963, Orbison came right back with **In Dreams,** another dream song, only this one was about a guy who awoke from his dream to find his girl was gone, and she wasn't coming back. We all went through it, so this one hit home.

While I can think, while I can talk, while I can stand, while I can walk; While I can dream, please let my dream come true, right now.

If you hear strains of Elvis again, **If I Can Dream** is the reason why. Although it's more a dream about peace than love, they go hand in hand, and that worked for me.

I dreamed a dream in time gone by, When hope was high and life worth living; I dreamed that love would never die, I prayed that God would be forgiving.

Was there ever a sadder song written about the dream of love than **I Dreamed a Dream**? This was an important one for me, because as it came along just as my heart had suffered a near-fatal break, and then arose from the ashes a few years later when I found an even more fulfilling love while she and I witnessed this song be sung while on a date to see **Les Miserables** on Broadway early in the Millennial year of 2000.

I was 54, and that was the night when — finally — I didn't need the dream anymore. It had become reality. Her name is Anne, and 2026 is our 26th year of a very loving marriage.

Explaining dreams can be like viewing the Northern Lights. Fascinating, but real?
Pixabay

27

Perchance Not to Dream

Recently, I was attacked in bed by three unknown, naked women who wanted my body.

Their ferocity and desperation scared the hell out of me and, contrary to what some guys might do, I fought them off savagely and — finally — successfully.

In my flailing about the bed, however, my left wrist bonked my wife on the head as she slept blissfully ignorant of my plight until my swinging arm found its unintended mark on the top of her skull.

Fortunately, no structural damage was done, but she obviously awoke with a start.

"Jim! For God's sake, what is going on?" she shouted. "You just hit me!"

Or at least that's what she told me later that she said. Having dived so deeply into my nightmare world, I was tuned completely out of the conscious one, so she resorted to shaking and banging *on me instead* to wake me up.

When I did come to, I was out of breath and dropped back onto my pillow to find my focus. When the fog cleared, I immediately apologized to Anne, then again, and then again. And then a fourth time.

I told her what she already knew by then: I was having one of my "action dreams" wherein my body joined in with my *dreamself* and all hell broke loose beneath the sheets. Anne has seen this happen before with me.

Then, just two nights later, I was fighting off three very unsavory thugs who were attempting to kill me, and my left leg swung over my body to the right to kick one of them in the groin. That, however, propelled me out of bed where I hit the floor. My foot plowed into the wall instead of any assailants, and I smashed three of my toes.

(Maybe I just have an innate fear of the number *three?*)

Again, Anne awoke with a start and, again, reached across the bed to defend me from myself.

Welcome to my world of undisclosed drug side effects or, alternatively, some really wild drug interactions producing hallucinogenic episodes in my sleep.

I have always prided myself on staying away from pills — even prescribed ones — especially when they contain naproxen or oxycodone. Recent medical problems have necessitated taking some, however, as well as some fluoxetine, more commonly known as Prozac.

Since these phantom night strikes in bed have occurred, I have dropped the first two of these pills completely, and am now only on fluoxetine. I don't think that alone is causing any of these nighttime attacks, but the residue of the first two drugs may well be. I've known for years that naproxen can give me bad dreams, and I'm sure the pain pills do, too.

I've learned that each of us is the best arbiter of deciding when the pharmaceutical *cure* is worse than the malady for which we take it. And sometimes we just have to experience the effects first-hand to believe them.

But I do know now what to Get Anne for Christmas: A football helmet and pads.

Part of my sleep issues, however, are caused by going so far under, so quickly when I lay my head down at night. Anne has told me I'm the soundest sleeper she has ever seen. She insists it's not possible for someone to sleep through the things I have.

So, if I'm not diving into a dream, I am diving deeply into the world of REM sleep where even a home invader -- God forbid -- would have trouble waking me up to find out where we stash the cash.

On more than one occasion, I slept through earthquakes that shook our home in Southern California. On another occasion, I was just taking a nap on the 40th floor of a San Francisco hotel when I slept through most of another one. Imagine the top half of a high rise swaying back and forth in the night, and you have that hotel, with me in one of the highest rooms. The only thing that made me come to was the movement of my shaking bed. Even then, though, I just rolled over to chide my dog for jumping on the mattress. But I had no dog with me, and that thought woke me up in time to catch the last of the evacuees headed down the long flights of stairs to a safer level. Most elevators don't work well in the midst of a quake. And, even if they do, you're still better off on the stairs.

Anne's favorite tale that she loves to spin at parties is what she calls the *bunny saga*. We often sleep with our bedroom door ajar in the summer so our three dogs can go in and out when nature calls during the night. On one July night, however, we had a *visitor* from the backyard in the form of a rabbit. Our dogs were all over it like Winnie the Pooh on honey, chasing it through the bedroom, then down the hall and into the kitchen and the rest of the house.

Our Yoyo was bred for chasing rabbits.
Herbert Aust/Pixabay

Oh, and did I mention one of our three dogs is a Greyhound and used to do this for a living?

Anne was awake instantly to join the chase -- and try to protect the bunny -- but to no avail. The rabbit was screeching (or whatever rabbits call it), the dogs were barking, Anne was yelling at all of them and -- by the way -- at me, too.

Why me? Because I was sleeping soundly through the whole donnybrook.

The chaos was over in about 5 minutes, and it did not end well for the rabbit, sad to say. Or for me, either. My wife couldn't believe I could sleep so soundly and be oblivious to all that circus racket. Try as I might, I could not convince her I was not playing possum while the rabbit was escaping to his own long sleep across the rainbow bridge.

So, whether I'm dreaming or not as I slumber, I usually wake up refreshed although I'm not the most popular guy in the household.

Min and I quickly made up for lost time.

28

Love at First Sight

In 1988, my then-wife Diane and I decided we had deferred too long our decision to adopt children. We had let the love of our careers hold sway for the eight years we'd been married, and it was time to start growing our family alongside those careers.

Since it looked like we were unable to produce our own kids, we began our journey to adopt. We were living in Indianapolis, a city that was growing quite a nice population of South Korean orphans, so we began working with an agency that worked internationally.

One of the rules of the agency was there could be no more than forty years of age between either parent and the age of adopted child. Since I was already 42, that meant infant adoption was not possible. The child would have to be no younger than 2 years old. That was fine with us, and we began the process we thought would take up to a year.

Turns out, it would only take a couple months. The reason was there were several children between 4 and 8 years of age who were deemed "special needs" children. Usually that referred to various stages of disabilities, but not always. One night in July, while we looked through the faces and stories of the available children, our attention was drawn to a six-year-old boy who was standing straight as an arrow -- as if he were at attention -- carrying a stoic look and trying his best to look confident, and doing a good job at it.

This kid had absolutely nothing wrong with him, physically or otherwise, so I asked our adoption counselor why he was in this special needs book. The answer startled me:

"Because Min Jin is 6 years old," she said. "Whenever a child turns 6, they go into this book because they are usually harder to adopt."

Harder to adopt? This guy? That's crazy, I thought.

That boy was to become ours. We had zero doubts. If you can fall in love at first sight with someone via only a picture and short bio, then that's exactly what we did. Any kid who could hold his own and appear confident in the chaos of an orphanage ... well, we applied for him the next morning.

Min Jin was often called "Minyah" for his young age. Clearly, though, he was about to grow out of that name. To us, he just became Min, to which we added the American name of David, just in case he would find it helpful to have as he adjusted to life in the United States.

Within a week, we were told we could have him as our son. To say we were elated would be a gross understatement. We agreed to go to Seoul, South Korea, to meet him, stay a week in-country, and then bring him home to our home in Indianapolis. This trip would take place in September, and since this was also the year that Seoul was hosting the 1988 Summer Olympics, we would get to see some of that, as an added bonus. But the main event was meeting Min and bringing him to his new home.

That meeting came at the downtown Seoul offices of the Holt Adoption Agency, and it is a moment frozen in time, even though it happened almost 40 years ago now. Min entered the room, wearing a red pullover shirt and blue jean overalls. His deep black hair was tousled a bit, but he was trying for that brave stoicism that we saw in his picture weeks before.

I crouched down to his eye level and said, "Anyung, Min." He returned his hello and then, before I knew it, my arms were wrapped around him in an embrace that he did not resist at all.

We stayed with him in the room and let him open a couple presents we got for him. I think one was a remote controlled car because I'd heard his favorite TV show was the American-made *Knight Rider* who had an amazing talking car called "Kit." Kind of a modern-day Bat Car.

My wife was doing the same embracing of Min that I was, but we didn't want to scare him, so we decided to let the expressions of love develop slowly. We were both already in love with this kid and couldn't wait to bring him home.

The week passed quickly, we were able to see a couple of the Olympic volleyball games and have scheduled times to meet with Min at the orphanage. On that first meeting, we prepared by buying toys for all of the children in his unit, and joined them in playing basketball outside on the court. Such a wildly fun and meaningful day.

The orphanage had dressed Min in a traditional South Korean "hanbok," an elegant robe that bespoke his culture. It was Min's job to host us and the other orphans in his group for this special event which featured cake and ice cream and all the presents we brought for the kids. As much fun as the kids all seemed to have, I wondered how many of them were a little sad it was not they who were going home with their new family that day. And I wondered how many times Min himself had been in their shoes, watching and awaiting his turn.

Min, his new mom and me all arrived at the airport two mornings later to begin the long flight home, and the new phase of life for all of us began. It was to be a long, long flight with moments of heavy turbulence. But Min slept through most of it, and his new mom and I were entranced just watching him slumber.

We all made it home safely, and Min hit the ground running in America. He conquered the language and culture within several months. Early on, he also exhibited the drive and intelligence that would serve him well in life. I felt early on that this guy was a born salesman. For example, a couple months after living with us, he worked up a sales pitch to sell me a car even though he was ten years away from being able to drive.

His pitch was perfect, and I was impressed, even though the car he was selling me was my own. Nevertheless, I bought it on the spot, although he had to settle for Monopoly money in exchange. I think I went and bought him some McDonald's fries, too. His favorite meal.

Min took to America like a guy who had always dreamed of living here. In fact, this may have been the case since his favorite TV shows as a small child in South Korea were American shows. His favorite was the Knight Rider series and that great talking car Kitt. Min was a natural at making friends, and he had plenty of them in no time after he started school.

Fast forward to today, and Min is still thriving in the sales world. He chose my alma mater, the University of Oklahoma, to attend. He graduated in 2005, launched himself into a sales career and has been moving up the ladder ever since. Only this time, he is selling surgical equipment for one of the nation's largest medical manufacture and supply firms. The home he bought a few years back in Noblesville, Indiana, is twice the size of mine, and he has chosen the single life wherein the love of his life is his Husky Brodie.

Some of life's mysteries are absolutely wonderful. David Min is one of the best.

Father meets son in Seoul.

Kao and me at the Bangkok Airport, along with the doctor who saw us off, just before boarding the plane that took us home to America.

29

Checking Out of Hotel Reno

In 1990, we made the decision to try for a second international adoption. We wanted to get a brother for our 8-year-old Min who had been with us now for two wonderful years.

We were informed by our adoption counselor, however, that South Korea was less of an option now than in 1988. There were still plenty of orphans there, but the Korean government had decided to place more orphans in-country and slow down the pace of adopting to families in other countries.

Apparently, the 1988 Seoul Olympics had something to do with that decision. We were told that, among all the myriad of media stories aired about Korea during those games, several focused on the many international adoptions taking place there. Leaders felt this was not the image that a fully developed nation should present to the world. Such a country should not have to give up its children to other countries; they should show the world they could place their children in their home country. So, just like that, the Korean international adoption door had closed. At least for the time being.

My then-wife Diane heard of a medical doctor in Hawaii who was having success in getting orphans out of Cambodia, where he had a home and spent part of the year. He ran more of a freelance operation (there was no actual agency involved), but it was all legal. We contacted him and yes, there were children available for adoption from an orphanage in Phnom Penh. He sent us information and a photo of one young boy, age 6, named Kao Kuhn. Something about Kao struck a loving chord with us, and we said yes, we would like to adopt him.

Diane and I began making arrangements, but it would be expensive, and we would have to travel to Cambodia to meet the boy and bring him home to America. We learned that the process might seem more ambiguous than the traditional adoption was with Min in Korea. There could be some risks involved, so I felt I should go alone to Thailand, just in case.

A week later, the doctor called and we set up a day and time for me to fly to Bangkok and pick up Kao. Thailand would have to be where we'd meet because Cambodia was closed to American tourists at the time. Our meeting place was to be in Bangkok at the Hotel Reno. Well, I thought, good name, given this was to be a risky trip! But I followed his instructions, strapped several thousand dollars to my waist in a money belt, and headed for the Indianapolis Airport.

My plane touched down late the next night in Bangkok, and I took a taxi to the Hotel Reno, located down a dark, winding alley in the heart of this busy city. I checked into the hotel, asked the desk clerk what room the orphans were in, and he responded "Room 230. There are several of them there."

I walked to that room, knocked on the door, and a teenage caretaker opened it, smiled, and pointed across a room full of sleeping children to Kao, asleep on the floor. in the corner. I fell as much in love with him then as I had with Min two years earlier. I thought it best to let him sleep, go to my own room to sleep through the night and return the next morning to meet Kao and take him to breakfast. I asked the young caretaker if Kao had a suitcase, and he said, "No sir. All he has is what he's wearing." That was a tee-shirt, shorts, and sandals. And, since the shirt was two sizes too large, it was apparent even that was borrowed.

The caretaker then added his own request, and it was startling, given the size of the task I was already facing.

"If you wouldn't mind, Sir, we have one other young boy from the orphanage whose new parents will be a day late picking him up. Could you take him, too, for just a day until they arrive? We don't have anyone else to look out for him."

I said yes. How could I not?

The full weight of what Kao had faced thus far in his four years of life was now upon me. Dropped into an orphanage as an infant, having no one or nothing to call his own, growing up with an evolving cast of strangers who came and went, no formal education other than what survival teaches, the list went on and on. And now here he was, about to meet me -- a man from a different country who, although a total stranger, would be taking him somewhere far away, probably forever. How much was that to process for anyone? This little guy was so brave, and I vowed to myself to make it as easy on him as possible. It's just that I had no idea how to do that. I would start learning the next morning.

It was then, that first night in Bangkok, that I realized fully that this adoption trip might indeed be risky. I was relying on the doctor from Hawaii, whom I'd never met face-to-face, and who was a day late in showing up. I was alone in the strange country of Thailand I had never before visited. Neither I nor my new son were citizens of Thailand, we didn't speak the language, and yet I was somehow supposed to get him out of there and back to the states. I'll just have to figure it out as I go along, I thought.

The next morning, I met Kao at his room, and tried to make myself understood with a few words I'd learned of the Cambodian language. His young caretaker helped out with that, and Kao seemed calmer than I thought he would be. I think it helped that his young fellow orphan went with us to spend the day together. I took them both downstairs to breakfast, and I tried to think up things to do with them. The hotel had a pool, so I took them there. they could swim in their shorts, and they seemed up for that.

When we got to the pool, I realized how uninitiated to life his young friend was. The kid whose new parents would pick him up later walked up to the pool and, feeling the urge, dropped his shorts and peed right into the water of the shallow end of the pool that was now fully in use by others who sat there watching. I wished I'd known how to say, "He's not my kid," in their language, but I didn't. The moment passed and the boys started romping in the water with me playing lifeguard.

I had just gotten the two boys dried off from their swim when the other parents arrived to pick up their son and take him to his new home in Minnesota. Was I glad to see them? Yes. Did I tell them that their new son confuses swimming pools with toilets? No.

That afternoon, I took Kao across the street in Bangkok to a large department store. It was time to buy him his own clothes, and maybe a teddy bear to comfort him at night. Everything was new for him, starting with the escalators that we took to the third floor. Kao's eyes popped when he saw them, and was so excited to take the ride. As we approached the floor for kids clothes, Kao -- this kid who had grown up surrounded by the jungles of Cambodia, yells out, "MICKEY!" What the hell, I thought, and then I saw what he saw: a large display of Mickey Mouse featured in the children's department. Kao might not have known much, but he knew Mickey Mouse! So, the first thing I bought him was a set of Mickey Mouse pajamas. This kid was now ready to show his smile. And, probably for the first time ever, he had things to call his own, including a teddy bear and -- of course -- a stuffed plushy of Mickey Mouse.

Mercifully, the facilitating doctor would make his entry the next morning to get us through the embassy paperwork, and he apologized for being delayed. There were one or two snags, but we made it through the day successfully. We would be flying out the next morning, and I've never been happier to get on a plane, feel that plane shooting down the runway, and the hear the gears retract into the wheel wells as the aircraft rose into the sky, heading west to Tokyo and, then, America.

The next day, our plane touched down in Dallas, and then in Chicago where Diane and Min greeted us. It was December 23, and Kao was about to experience his first Christmas at his new home, with his new family. I'm sure it was one he has never forgotten.

I will leave it to the following song lyrics I wrote a few months later to summarize what happened in that Thai capital city. If you'd like to hear what this song sounds like, you can locate the playlist on my *Windward319 YouTube channel*, look for "Hotel Reno," and listen.

Today, our kindhearted and loving Kao is a graduate of Indiana University and a practicing nurse. He is married and lives in the Indianapolis area. We are so proud of him and love him very much. I can't imagine how my life would have been without John Kao in it.

Now, here is that story, in song lyrics:

Hotel Reno

On a plane bound for Thailand
Flying from Texas,
I was going to help my son
Break free.
From four years of hardship
And four years of a child's wish
For love, peace, security
And family.

Touchdown in Bangkok,
I hit the midnight streets
And sidewalks,
Looking for the place
Where he would be;
In a city known for danger,
The only thing I wanted
Was a kid named Kao
To break free
And go with me.

Turned left into an alley,
A real urban valley,
A place where tourists
Seldom go;
And there in the dark,
I met this gambler named Kao
Upstairs in Room 230,
Hotel Reno.

The kid was asleep
On the floor in a T-shirt,
That draped his body
Like a sack;
But peace draped his face
And a hope he'd escape
From this hunger
And never look back;
Could it be like that?

But the way out of Bangkok
Was littered with roadblocks
For a young, brave orphan at best;
And just as it seemed,
We would not break free,
From his past that had
Put him to the test...
Our plane headed west.

Now high in the sky,
I look down at my side
At Kao asleep as we go,
The T-shirt is gone,
He has Mickey Mouse on
And he remembers the
Gamble that he'd known:
Hotel Reno.

On a plane bound for Texas
Flying from Thailand,
With the Bangkok casino
Just a dream,
Kao awakes,

He has a smile on his face,
And he feels
An American breeze.
Kao is free.

Beginnings don't define us
But beginnings can inspire us,
And today, Kao is a man;
He has a spirit to help others
As a nurse and as a brother,
As a son and as a family man,
He's shown he can!

The Willis boys today (Kao left, Min right), charging ahead and loving life.

International students can benefit from homestay parents.
Pixabay

30

The Win-Win of Homestay Parenthood

For eight of our 25 married years, Anne and I have lived apart for much of each year, due to the two-career marriage rules.

We are not just talking different cities or adjoining states. During those years, we have commuted *across country*. Like, 2,000 miles of it.

First, from California to Ohio, then from California to Kentucky. As I look back on it, I'm not sure how we pulled that off, but we did.

One thing that helped was filling our house with visiting international students at nearby Ashland University, where Anne taught English as a second language. We were designated "homestay parents" for as many as five of these college students, and it gave Anne a lot of company while I was gone. It allowed me to feel more secure about her safety at home, too.

Turns out, a lot of other couples have, commuter marriages too. In fact, data shows that 3.5 million married couples live and work apart in 2026. That is *double* the number of commuter marriages in 1990. Demographically , almost all commuter couples are very well educated and are holding professional or executive positions. Many of these professionals are in higher education. More than half have been married at least 10 years.

Surprising to some people is the fact that commuter couples do *not* have a higher divorce rate than non-commuters. Anne and I fit right in with these statistics and hit on all their cylinders. Despite the time apart, we're still together and deeply committed to each other.

A few years back, we heard entertainer Dolly Parton quip in one of her concerts about her own commuter marriage of 58 years to the late Carl Dean.

"I was on the road so much, year in and year out," she said, "but Carl and I actually think being apart is one reason we've been married so long!"

Anne and I have joked about the same thing, and there's some truth to it. While neither of us likes the idea of being apart, it does allow two professionals to focus on the work they love, exercise the personal independence that co-dependent couples don't have, and it makes those reunions and homecomings so much more fun and romantic!

Anne and I don't have kids together, and our young ones from previous marriages are all grown and have their own families. I know the long-term commuter marriage would have been infinitely harder if we'd had kids at home.

One other thing also helped make it doable, and it's cited in the couples' demographics earlier: at least one of us, and sometimes both, have had careers in higher education during the commuting periods. That did not make us smarter; it just put us both on college academic calendars throughout the year.

Because we didn't teach summers and because we had long breaks at Christmas, plus spring and fall breaks, we had a lot of time to see each other that other commuting couples couldn't have. That helped immensely.

Then there was the knowledge that I didn't leave Anne in an empty Ohio house while I was in California. Not by the longest shot. She had the company of our three dogs and three cats, and also of a half-dozen college students for whom she was "house mom."

No, we didn't live in a university Greek house, but we did welcome international students into our home to live while they studied English from Anne at Ashland University in Ohio. They all called her *Mom* (except for our Korean Richard, who kept addressing her as *"Anne Willis"*).

Officially these were "homestay students," but unofficially they were our extended family.

It was a comfort for me in California to know that, should a burglar try foolishly to break into our large home on the heavily treed Ridgewood Court, he'd have a bloody brawl on his hands. And he would lose.

Five strapping guys (Sultan, Richard, Robert, Jack and Willy), three large and loud dogs (Maggie, Shadow, and Charlie), and three no-nonsense women students (Amy, Emily, and Sherry). And of course, Anne herself who, with her "I-don't-think-so" spirit, is not one to mess with.

Not that life with this bunch was always a picnic. It might have helped if everyone came from the same country, but they didn't.

Our kids were from across Asia and the Middle East. Three were from China, one from Taiwan, one from Japan, two from South Korea, and one from Saudi Arabia.

A few memories might depict what a circus our home was at times (and why I was not *too* unhappy then about being 2000 miles away):

- Dinner time. Hard to get everyone to eat the same thing. Some didn't eat pork, some didn't eat beef, and some ate too much of everything for the size of the meal budget. Since Anne did much of the grocery shopping and cooking, she bore the brunt of figuring it all out.

- Sultan. We could write a book just about him. Nice guy, but he was the privileged son of a high-ranking Saudi general and had servants doing basically everything for him at home. Once, he wandered into the kitchen and announced to Anne he'd *never been in one*, and asked where the refrigerator was, even though he was standing right in front of it. He also needed a tutorial on how to use the microwave. Sultan would prepare grocery lists for her that included items like "rostbif," *"brid"* and (ready for it?) *"Diet Cocks."* Anne still laughs over the latter and had no idea what "brid" was until Sultan's English improved enough to say "bread." Rostbif was a little easier: roast beef. He never did manage "Diet Cokes," though.

- Sultan and Robert didn't get along, but thank God for Robert assuming the role of Sultan's older and smarter brother. Sultan was so lazy he would oversleep constantly. When Anne was ready to haul the students to school in the morning, Sultan was still in bed. Finally, Robert got so pissed he went into Sultan's adjoining room, reached over and shook him, shouting, *"Sultan!!* You are a naughty boy! Get your butt up and get downstairs. Your father would be ashamed!" That did the trick. It wasn't enough to save Sultan's cushy home, though. Anne, Robert (and

I think the rest of the students) agreed it was time for him to find other living quarters. So, Sultan moved closer to campus and eventually graduated. Maybe taking care of himself caused him to grow up?

- Richard didn't like Sherry, who lived in our walkout lower level. I think it was a cross-cultural thing: Korean vs. Japanese. He often complained to Anne about Amy (when it was usually Richard who'd been wrong) and refused to call her by name. Instead, he opted for "that girl who lives in the basement."
- Richard again. No matter what Anne was doing at night, Richard was always under his nose wanting homework help. *"Anne Willis,* you must help me with this," he would plead. Usually, Anne took time from her work to do it.

But there were the sweet memories, too.

Jack, who became a born-again Christian in Ashland, would go for walks throughout the neighborhood, singing hymns of praise. He loved talking with Anne's 3-year-old granddaughter Kyah, who loved Jack and still today boasts about "teaching Jack his colors."

Robert, who is Chinese, was the opposite of Sultan in terms of efficiency. He wound up completing a two-year MBA in one year, and he would often fill his free time by helping around the house. He loved washing Anne's car for her out in the driveway and, one morning did it during freezing weather at 6:30 a.m. And, while Jack became an evangelical Christian, Robert became a Mormon while living with us. I remember his girlfriend having a lot to do with that.

Happily, all our students graduated from their respective programs at the university, and all became fluent in English, thanks to Anne. So, what had begun as just a commuter marriage for us, expanded into an unforeseen opportunity. We were able to offer a fairly normal family life for six strangers who became our homestay family who had been cut off by thousands of miles from their own moms and dads.

Such is the mystery of life, and such is the wonder of my wife.

Does a movie really end when the credits roll?
Pixabay

31

A Dress Rehearsal for Life

My wife Anne tells me often how amazed she is that I can recall scenes from movies, and the dialogue that goes with them, as easily as I do. I sometimes counter with how easily she can identify a couple bars of a classical music piece and know what key signature it's done in.

To me, there is no difference between what I do and what she does. We are both reacting to *art* that has inspired us to the point of remembering it down to its tiny details.

The art of abstracting

But I like to do more than remember scenes and dialogue from films, I look for ways to abstract from them to real life. It seems natural to match those artistic renderings to actual *lifescenes* that I find myself confronting and or/see others living through. When I find those parallels, I often relate a movie scene to it.

For one thing, it helps me feel that others have faced such situations and survived. Even if it did happen in the movie. When my frontal lobe's *amygdala* alerts me to a dangerously familiar situation, I start thinking about the movie *Jaws II,* when Sheriff Martin Brody warns the doubting mayor of Amity that he has another shark problem on his hands. The veteran shark killer goes eyeball to eyeball with the mayor and explodes, "I've seen a shark up close, and you'd better do something about *this* one because I don't intend to go through that hell again!"

And, of course, that's exactly what Brody winds up doing.

Pain avoidance

Most of us have had our own version of shark moments in the past which have probably produced a certain level of PTSD. And we find Brody's fiery warning fits how much we want to avoid any such future hell. We become one with the good sheriff of Amity.

Anne has heard me utter some of favorite movie lines many times, and she can recognize which line is coming, based on the situation at hand. Sometimes, for instance, when a situation dictates I do something unpleasant (which I may bristle at, even though I was actually planning to do anyway), I remember a scene from *Shane.* It's where farmer Joe Starrett (Van Heflin) mistakes a drifting Shane (Alan Ladd) as an adversary and tells him to get off his land.

Shane balks a moment and Starrett asks, "What's the difference? You're leaving anyway." To which Shane replies, "I'd like it to be *my* idea."

Anne has lost track of the number of times she's heard me say that.

Invoking the arts

These are but two of dozens of times I've invoked scenes and dialogues from films to point out the parallels between art and daily life, and how these films may show us what is undergirding the words and actions of real-life people in real-life conflicts.

To me, the entertainment aspect of good films is only part of their value. Like anyone else, I can easily be persuaded to spend 20 bucks to go see what promises to be an exciting story unfold on the big screen. But the added value of many such movies is the *roadmap* they can provide for similar situations we may encounter myself in real life.

When I taught ethics at the university level, I often assigned students the task of finding films that illustrated the ethical principles we were discussing, and to show those clips and explain their relevance in class.

I would explain that storytelling in films (like all good art) can be a kind of *dress rehearsal* for life.

In her book, *Seeking Goodness and Beauty,"* editor Patricia Lamoureux writes her first chapter on "The Formative Power of Story." She explains that arts can help us see morality and ethics directly and indirectly. They can bring us to Tolstoy's nagging question, "What then must we *do?*"

Familiar question

Incidentally, that same question is uttered by the character Billy Kwan (Linda Hunt playing a man) in the film, *The Year of Living Dangerously*. Kwan is desperately trying to show journalist Guy Hamilton (a young Mel Gibson) why he needs to focus on the oppressed *people* in Jakarta rather than on the politicians in the palace.

Lamoureux explains that the arts can invite us to reflect on how we are forming ourselves in the midst of cultural pressures that are also trying to form us. In Hamilton's case, he was fighting the peer pressure of other journalists who saw Indonesia's problems as just another political conflict and not a situation in which people were starving and dying.

Tour Guides

If we let them, the arts can work as a tour guide through life's thorny and treacherous paths, and they can do it on three levels: through our perception of how the film or literary characters are behaving, through imaginative identification with these characters, and through the level of discernment where we ask ourselves if they are doing the right thing or not. And, if not, how should they — indeed, how should I — do it?

Values and cannoli

I would add that a good writer can show us — sometimes in a humorous way — how we prioritize things strangely in life, including life itself. And here I go again with a parallel from a movie, in this case the quote-laden film, *The Godfather.*

I'm thinking of the scene where Paulie is assassinated in his car and gangster Peter Clemenza, who set it up, tells the killer Rocco, "Leave the gun. Take the cannoli."

Of course, the scene can also show how whacked out our priorities can get.

The neon lights are bright on Broadway.
Vinsky/Pixabay

32

Those Magical Musicals

As I think about my love for live theater, two musicals come to mind. They stand out not only because they were wonderful shows, but also because of the impact they had on people I was with when I saw them: people I cared about.

The first, chronologically, was *A Chorus Line*, and the second was *Les Miserables*.

The big trip

It was the fall of 1979, and I was teaching journalism at the University of Missouri. I had volunteered to be the adviser of the U of M Chapter of The society of Professional Journalists, which then was known as Sigma Delta Chi. Each year the SPJ holds an annual convention for both students and working journalists, and this year it was in New York City.

I had 10 eager students who wanted to go, but who were also low on disposable income. So to keep costs low, I agreed to drive them to New York in a large university van. We were on the road for 20 hours and pulled into Manhattan early in the morning for our stay at the Waldorf Astoria Hotel, which was the convention hotel.

"One" for the ages

It was the first time any of us had been to the Big Apple, and we were blown away by everything we saw, most notably the musical that first night. It was *A Chorus Line*, and it had us in its grip from the opening number, *"I Hope I Get It,"* right down through *"What I Did for Love"* and the reprise of *"One."*

This landmark show, which won multiple Tony Awards plus a Pulitzer Prize for drama, had already been running for four years at the Shubert Theater and would go on to become the seventh longest running show in Broadway history. The music was by Marvin Hamlisch, lyrics by Edward Kleban, and the book was written by James Kirkwood Jr. and Nicholas Dante.

A real education

The students were spellbound throughout the production, and I realized how important this trip would be for their education. We crammed so much into our three-day stay in New York, but *A Chorus Line* would emerge as the crown jewel, according to a brief survey I conducted with the kids before we left town.

I lost track of the number of times they spontaneously broke into *"One"* on the drive back to Columbia, Missouri.

Fast-forward 20 years to the spring of 2000. It was the first year of the 21st Century, and I was in New York City to meet my new friend, Anne, who would become my wife in a few more months. This was only our third date, however, and we were getting to know each other slowly since we had both been burned by previous relationships.

So, beyond a couple of good-night hugs, our friendship had thus far produced no touching. I felt as nervous about reaching out to her as I had on my awkward dates back in high school.

I had seen *Les Mis* in Indianapolis a few years before, loved it, and I wanted Anne to see it. The show would wind up being the sixth longest-running musical on Broadway.

Channeling "Sleepless"

Anne was staying with a friend in Long Island, and I met her at Grand Central Station earlier in the afternoon. Our one-two punch as tourists consisted of a walk to the Empire State Building where we saw the city from the observation deck (ala Tom Hanks and Meg Ryan), followed by going to see *Les Mis,* with a dinner at a quaint theater district cafe squeezed in between.

As we strolled from the cafe to the theater, I broke through my doubt about touching Anne. I didn't want to seem too presumptuous, but it felt like the time was right.

The big touch

I prefaced my touch by saying, "I'd better hold on to you, Annie, because I wouldn't want to lose such a pretty woman to some vagabond on these city streets!"

With that preamble, I reached out and found a welcoming hand reaching back, and it felt like first-time love all over again.

We found the Broadway Theater, took our seats, and I felt the same enthralling grip from the opening numbers of *Les Mis* that I had felt in *A Chorus Line* two decades before. Only this time, that grip was tighter because of the woman sitting next to me, and because the casual hand-holding we felt on our walk to the theater had become a vise grip involving all four of our hands.

We were so close to each other, I wondered for a moment why I had even bothered to buy two seats.

A show of magic

The words and music of *Les Miserables* had helped Anne and me overcome our initial fear of getting involved again, and transported us — right in that theater — to the next level, which has now become a 26-year marriage.

The show's lyrics had a lot to do with that. *"I Dreamed a Dream," and "One Day More"* were words and phrases that took on new meaning for us that night, as Annie and I each realized neither of us was no longer *"On My Own."*

Ever wonder who the most worn out one is after a ballgame? It's probably the baseball itself.

Wokandapix/Pixabay

33

A Moment of His Own

When Evelyn, an outfielder for the Rockford Peaches women's baseball team in the 1940s, misses a throw to the cutoff player, manager Jimmy Dugan (played wonderfully by Tom Hanks) unloads on her in a string of very vocal invectives.

He is not a happy man, but he knows he has a very sensitive Evelyn on his hands who he must chew out. The emotional restraint he tries to produce for her -- while still lambasting her -- is hilarious.

Screaming, "Who's team are you playing for?!" he reduces the young woman to tears. Evelyn's reaction leaves a stunned Jimmy bellowing, *"Are you crying?!"* He follows it immediately with one of the classic lines of filmdom:

"There's no crying in baseball!"

A problem guy

Dugan, a lead character in the film, *A League of Their Own,* is a case study of a guy with a short fuse. quickened even more by frustration and alcohol. Happily, for his players, he learns to lay off the booze and get a handle on his anger.

The scene where he first does the latter nearly causes him to implode. It also provides one of the funniest moments of this classic movie.

When Evelyn makes the same throwing error again, he signals with a summoning index finger for her to see him as the inning ends. Evelyn is full of trepidation, and Jimmy is trying mightily (yet visibly) to keep his emotional volcano from exploding. His entire body is in a state of tremor.

Steam rises

He begins his speech in a wordless manner as his hands do the talking while he twists his face into a pained smile inches from her face. Then he says in a forced, hushed tone, *"You ... missed ... the ... cutoff ... again. Is that ... something ... you could work on? Thank you."*

His faux smile and the lack of vocal vitriol makes a genuine smile come to Evelyn's face as she realizes Jimmy is trying to be nice. She knows she has just dodged a hand grenade and merrily runs back to the dugout.

I've seen this movie at least 10 times, and each time I realize how hard it was for Jimmy Dugan to tame his inner tiger at that moment. Once done, however, it seemed easier for him to handle the team of professional women baseball players he had been handed. And to win more games to boot.

A real struggle

As one prone to anger in his younger years, I understand the process Jimmy was going through. It was a painful, belated, growing-up experience for him. It's a process that doesn't work for all anger-prone adults, and it took time for me to get on the other side of it.

We can all learn something from a character portrayal like Jimmy Dugan. We can learn that, no matter what our age, our anger issues have not necessarily kept up with our calendar age. It's something we have to realize is a problem, and then we have work to do in overcoming that angry display.

Still, as was the case with Jimmy Dugan, the resulting life just seems more peaceful without the pyrotechnics.

And, who knows? Maybe that peace helps keep crying out of baseball.

34

Tom Wingo, Dr. Sandhu, and Me

Tom Wingo found his peace in returning to his tidal basins of South Carolina. I found mine in going home to Oklahoma.

Pixabay

I have a lot in common with Tom Wingo.

"I am a teacher, a coach, and a well loved man. And that is more than enough."

— Pat Conroy, *The Prince of Tides.*

In the mid-1980s, I was living in Boston and teaching at Northeastern University, coaching my students on how to become better writers. I was also dealing with some anger issues that never produced physical violence to others, as they were more directed inward toward me. But the anger had a way of spilling out, often to those closest to me. That didn't make sense to me.

Until it did. For that, I can think Dr. H.S. Sandhu.

My inward anger also didn't make me much of a person to be around at the time, so I decided to do something about it.

What I did was to start consulting with a gifted psychotherapist in Boston, where I was living and working as a professor at Northeastern University. That's where Dr. Sandhu came in. He was with Boston University Hospital, and he followed the thinking of Freud, so Mom became a regular person of interest for us in our visits.

News to me

Still, since I was in my 40s at the time and my folks were living more than a thousand miles away, I had assumed that none of my issues were related to them. I felt we always had a close family, although I did know Mom often exhibited bipolar symptoms.

Once, on Christmas day as our guests were just taking their first bites of Mom's cooking, she stood up and announced, "Well I'm sorry you don't like it! Someone else can cook next time!" And then she marched right out of the den, into her bedroom, and slammed the door.

We all sat there in silence wondering what could have prompted that.

My role?

I somehow felt it was my role to fix what got broken in such times, but I was never sure how to or *why* it was my job.

So there was a fair amount of anger stored up, and I directed it at myself for not being more of a fixer.

Sandhu and I were making progress in Boston now, and I came to a point of realizing I had some work to do in standing on my own, without Mom's still-intact influence. My love for her, her love for me, and the fact I'd put her on a pedestal were blocking out some honest reflection on her influence. I discovered there was no need to defer to it in my adult life. I could write my own script from now on, and I could do it by myself.

Along comes a book

So it was that, in 1986, a book called **Prince of Tides** was published. I knew of its author, Pat Conroy, having already read **The Great Santini,** about the heavy-handed way in which a Marine officer dealt with his older son and wife. In *Tides,* Conroy decided to set his sights on the relationship of a *mother* and her son. Like *Santini,* it was also set in South Carolina, but quickly jumped to New York City for most of the book. Tom had gone there to help his sister Savannah, who had just tried to commit suicide. In so doing, he met her psychiatrist, Dr. Susan Lowenstein, and wound up learning as much about himself and how he and his sister had been under the influence of the same emotional trauma.

The paperback was over 700 pages long, a daunting length. But once I got into it, I could not put it down. I felt it was describing my relationship with my own mother, although Tom Wingo knew his mom was off the rails, while I still believed mine to be a saint.

Turns out, as is often the case, the truth was somewhere in the middle.

Not a saint after all

Mom was *human,* which meant flawed. She also loved me dearly, but she was dealing with her own longstanding insecurities about herself which sometimes prevented her from being the mom she wanted to be.

Since both Tom Wingo and I were seeing a psychiatrist at the same time and both talking about our moms, I felt a special attachment to him and his story. I was getting a lot from visits with Sandhu, but I found myself getting just as much from *Prince of Tides.*

Once I realized that Mom was only a mom and not Athena, the Goddess of Wisdom, and that she herself was the victim of her own parental chain reaction, I quit blaming her for my own issues.

It was time to take responsibility for me now.

That's when fate intervened, and I wound up back in my boyhood home of Oklahoma. It was in the spring of 1995, I was on leave from my faculty post at Boston College. While I was there, Timothy McVeigh blew up the Oklahoma City Federal Building, and I returned to the streets as a reporter for several weeks. That gave me time with my folks who lived in neighboring Midwest City, and I wound up having some good talks with my mom about things that had been bothering me about us.

An added bonus of that trip was that it reconnected me to both my hometown and state. I felt a bonding that I had not felt my growing-up years there.

Coupled with the work that Sandhu and I were doing in Boston on the same issues, it all helped bring both me and Mom some long-sought transparency with each other. I felt more peace, and I hope she did, too.

Comes fatherhood

More enlightenment about parenthood came when my then-wife and I adopted our first two sons and I became a dad. I began understanding the challenges of parenthood even better, and gave Mom credit for doing as good as she knew how. And, you know what? It was pretty good, after all.

In helping to raise David Min and John Kao, I learned that parents and kids all learn together in this learning curve called familyhood. Parenthood may come with instruction found in bookstores, but reading about how to do something the right way (if there is such a thing) and doing it, are two different things.

I know my boys' mother and I learned that parenting goes through cycles, from highs to lows and in-betweens, and that some of it has to do with what other pressures you are experiencing at the time, or that you have experienced long ago.

The latter is what Tom Wingo and I were dealing with. We had just chosen to cover it up, figuring it couldn't possibly still be affecting us.

In *The **Prince of Tides***, Tom (Nick Nolte) is led from darkness to light by his psychiatrist, (Barbra Streisand.) The film, which reduced me to tears as these characters came to life on the screen, hit home just as the book had.

So much so that I went back and re-read all 700+ pages again. In between, I saw the movie. A number of times, actually. I felt like author Pat Conroy had introduced me to my male kindred spirit, my alter ego, in this Tom Wingo character. Watching him find peace made me more determined to do it.

Sandhu vs. Streisand

I mentioned seeing the film to Sandhu, and I expected some insightful, clinical evaluation of it, since I thought he had seen it, too.

What I got instead was, *"Yeah, I liked it. But Tom's psychiatrist had better looking legs than mine."*

I figured that if *this* was the response my psychiatrist felt was most appropriate, he must have thought I was cured.

I don't know about Sandhu's legs, but I do know he helped me save my life. Along with Pat Conroy and Tom Wingo, of course.

35

OU Football, Jay, and Me

In the year 2000-2001, I accepted an invitation to become the McMahon Centennial Chair of Journalism at my alma mater, the University of Oklahoma. I was happy to come back to the campus that held so many good memories for me since my graduation there in 1968.

But I also learned the meaning of the phrase, "No one steps into the same river twice, because the waters are always moving." Such was also the case when I realized the

Jay Smith adorns the cover of our book.
Jim Willis

school was not the same one I'd left. That doesn't mean it wasn't good; it was. But it was just different. Different feelings, much more diverse geographically and in other way since 1968.

A lot of the old haunts, beer and pizza parlors that were permanent fixtures in my memory, were not replaced by new hangouts.

I was pondering one day in late August in my office when there was a rap on my door. I got up and opened it to find a giant of a man standing on the other side. His name was Jay Smith, and he was an offensive lineman for the OU football team. He was dressed nicely, had a warm smile, and stuck out his hand to introduce himself.

"I understand you write books, Dr. Willis. Is that right?"

"Yes, Jay, I've written several. "Come on in. What can I do for you?"

He came in and took one of my two visitor's chairs, emptying his 280-pound frame into the seat. Jay was big, but not fat. He was well groomed and had a very likable personality.

"Well," he said, "I've got a story to tell, and I'm looking for a writer to help me tell it. I was an "O" lineman for the Sooners for the past six years. I had a redshirt year, and then an injury year when I tore two Achilles tendons. So, the four years I played, I started each one."

"Impressive," I said. "So, obviously, you've played for a couple different coaches."

I was a big Sooner fan myself, and knew that OU had had a revolving door in the coach's position the past few years since Barry Switzer and the school agreed to part company.

"Yes, that's right," Jay said. "And that's part of what makes my story unique. During my six years at OU, I've played under four different head coaches and six different offensive coordinators. I've loved my time with the team, but it has not been easy, proving myself each year to a new coach. Still, I was always a starter in each of the four years I could play."

"Wow," I rejoined. "That was definitely not easy."

"Right. Then there was the matter of our win-loss record which was pretty abysmal, and didn't turn around until last year. As you know, the Sooners are used to winning; not losing. Our 5-5-1 record two years ago under Coach (Howard) Schnellenberger was an example of how bad it got. And that was the year we were supposed to win the national championship!"

Jay told me he was a blue chip player out of a high school football factory in Arlington, Texas, and that he had several top offers from schools, but chose OU because he felt they had turned the corner and were on an upward trajectory.

"But that turned out to be wishful thinking," he said. "Instead, I walked into a buzz saw with new coaches practically every year. I tried my best, but I wound up tearing both Achilles, and my promise a top draft pick in the pros didn't materialize. No team wants a guy with vulnerable ankles."

As I listened to Jay describe his life, a story arc started appearing to me, and I felt it would make a good book. We agreed I would approach a publisher I knew, then set up a meeting with all three of us. All of that happened quickly since the publisher was right on campus (the OU Press), the director liked the book idea, and we had signed a contract within a couple weeks.

Jay and I agreed to meet for me to interview him at least once weekly, and he supplied me with press materials he had about his OU career. We also agreed I would be the principal writer and that I would write it through Jay's eyes. He would be the first person narrator, but the words and structure would come from me. That is typical in sports memoirs.

We began our interviews on the first week of football season. We would meet on Fridays and I'd gain insight into his career, and then we'd turn around and watch the Sooners play the next day. The team was coming off its best season in five years, under a new head coach named Bob Stoops. Their record the previous year was 7-4, and the team had gone to the Independence Bowl. There was cautious optimism about this 2000-20001 football campaign.

So, we started the interviews, and a curious think happened alongside them: the Sooners began winning, and they kept on winning, Saturday after Saturday. By the time Bowl Season rolled around, OU was undefeated and was slated to play for the national championship in the Orange Bowl against favored Florida State. The Sooners won that game, 13-2, and won the national title.

Come January, Jay and I had done most of our interviews, and the Sooners had a new championshp trophy in their Athletic Department case.

A few months later, our book was done. We called it, "Prelude to Greatness: Sooner Football in the 1990s," but had to wait another several months for it to roll off the OU presses. Jay and I were both pleased with it and the story it told.

Here is an excerpt from that book:

On November 11, 1995, the storied Oklahoma football program hit rock bottom.

The Sooners had just lost to Oklahoma State, 12-0, in Normal to finish the season at 5-5-1 under first-year coach Howard Schnellenberger. That was the season we were supposed to win the national championship.

the day started with the coach's delivery of an incoherent radio interview and ended with a locker room fight. In between, the senior-laden Sooners made enough mistakes on defense to last a season and were unable to score even with a first and goal from the OSU 4-yard-line.

This was near the end of my second year or redshirt freshman season at OU. My parents had driven to Normal from Arlington, Texas, to watch the game in which I hoped the Sooners would score enough to get me into the game. My folks had made reservations at a local motel and were planning to spend the weekend in Norman.

But after the game, I was in shock. When I came out of the locker room, I asked them if we could get as far away as possible. So my parents canceled their room, and we drove back to Arlingon.

During the long drive home, I kept asking myself, "What happaned?"

I was one of the most highly recruited offensive linemen in the country, and I picked Oklahoma over 25 other schools because I loved OU, and its football program was returning to power. In the process, I left behind offers from other programs like Florida State, Nebraska, Texas, Notre Dane, and Alabama to name a few.

I thought things would be better at OU now. But I was wrong. Another five years of bad luck and losing lay ahead ..."

36

You're a Good Man, C.B.!

We all grew up with the iconic Charlie Brown of "Peanuts" Fame.
Michelle Raponi/Pixabay

My introduction to comedy came through what we called the "funny pages" of the morning or evening newspaper.

The best day of the week for those was, of course, Sundays. That's when a whole color comic *section* was added to that bulky weekly paper that took a muscular paperboy/girl to deliver by hand to the doorstep. Throwing it was akin to slinging a 15-pound bag of dog food across the yard.

By noontime, after church, pages of that brightly colored Sunday section would be all over the living room as we took turns sharing different strips in the family.

The 1950s Comics

My earliest memories were of cartoons like *Beetle Bailey, Blondie, Archie, Nancy, Mutt and Jeff,* and the one that outlived most of them, **Peanuts,** which lasted until the turn of the millennium, the year 2000.

Most people don't know that Charles Schulz had been writing that comic strip since 1947, although it appeared under the name of ***"Li'l Folks"*** until 1950. Those four original characters were Charlie Brown, Patty, Shermy, and Snoopy, who was silent (no thought balloons) until 1952 and who didn't walk upright until 1956. Lucy, who was the older sister of Linus and Rerun, first appeared in 1952.

C.B.: The reluctant star

Creator Schulz had a lot to say about the Peanuts characters over the years, including this about Charlie Brown: "He's a caricature. We all know what it's like to lose, but Charlie Brown keeps losing outrageously. it's not that he's a loser; he's really a decent little sort."

The thing I always noticed about that, though, is that C.B.'s friends never deserted him and always seemed to see him as a leader, reluctant though he was and ill-fated though his plans often were.

They liked him for who he was as a guy; not for what he did. And besides, who else would Lucy torment by pulling the football away at the last possible second before his kick?

Snoopy

About Snoopy, Schulz said, "Snoopy was the slowest to develop, and it was his walking around on two feet that eventually turned him into a lead character." Schulz even created a parallel universe in which Snoopy could operate. That setting was World War I, where the hound was an ace Air Corps pilot astride his doghouse taking off to face the enemy. He was usually either shooting it out with the cursed Red Baron, or scuttling across the ground on his belly, trying to escape the enemy after being shot down over France.

Often he was drowning his sorrows in Root Beer in a Paris cafe before taking his doghouse to the night sky once again. His doghouse never ran out of gas.

Linus, Lucy, and Sally

The character of Linus, who was Lucy's brother, was a close confidant and friend to Charlie Brown. His blanket became his trademark, an element Schulz said came from his own blanket-toting children. The innocence of Linus and his great heart helped make his belief in the Great Pumpkin believable to readers.

About Lucy, he said, "Lucy is the part of me who is capable of saying mean, sarcastic things. It's nice to have someone who can do that. Yet Lucy also has her softer, vulnerable side." She gets to rag on her friends — most notably Charlie Brown — through her guise as a sidewalk psychiatrist operating out of a booth that looks a lot like a neighborhood lemonade stand. That was, by the way, a setting we kids were intimately familiar with in the 1950s.

The character of Sally (C.B.'s brother) didn't appear until 1959. Schulz found she resonated a lot with girl readers. "Sally stands for all the frustration and confusion that little kids experience at school," he wrote. "She is a favorite of so many people because she is so uninhibited."

Witty and wise

Like so many of my generation who grew up with this cast of characters, which just kept growing to include even a tiny bird named Woodstock, I found reading *Peanuts* to be a must start to my daily *routine.*

And, like many other adults, I've discovered the wisdom found in the strip — what Schulz called "The Gospel According to Peanuts" — to be a useful guide to living life. That didn't mean things would always work out right but, hey, you still have your dog, right?

And besides, as one of the wittiest lines from the Peanuts strip says, in detracting us from gloom, *"Don't worry about the world coming to an end today, Charlie Brown. "It's already tomorrow in Australia."*

37

I Miss the Unity that Came with the News

I was a senior in high school when John F. Kennedy was assassinated. We got the news of his shooting during my journalism class when our teacher, Mrs. Householder, announced it and turned on the TV.

A silence descended on the classroom as a sadness arose from the dozen or so of us who were there. Quickly we were all locked in to what

A family in 1963 watches the story about President Kennedy's assassination.

Pixabay

the go-to news anchor of the day, Walter Cronkite, was telling us.

As journalism students, some of us were paying as much attention to *how* the event was being covered as we were what was happening. Mrs. Householder knew this could be a learning experience, and she suggested specific things we should look for in the reporting.

Shock and Awe

I don't remember much of that exercise in reverse engineering, and I can't believe I was too engaged in it at the moment. Most of us were in shock. Although we were in the middle of red-state Oklahoma, we were young and had warmed up to the idealism of this young president.

In 2013, however, I was asked to deliver a presentation at Massachusett's Worcester Polytechnic Institute in a 50th anniversary symposium on the JFK assassination.

I called my presentation, "The Media as a Unifier in Times of Grief." It focused on the display of unity in America over Kennedy's death. We were bound together by the strap and buckle of news. And much of that unity, short-lived though it may have been, was attributed to the excellent media coverage of it, plus the fact that most Americans were watching and hearing the same messenger bring us the news.

A Common Pool of Facts

That news outlet was CBS News, and that anchor was Mr. Cronkite. It was this common pool of information that was not only available to everyone with a TV in 1963, but was also heavily accessed by a great majority of Americans.

We were not only paying attention; we were hanging on every word, every kibble and bit of information we could get. We weren't looking around for countless other channels of news that would be in synch with our political beliefs, because there were none.

There was just CBS, NBC, and ABC. And, of those three, CBS and Cronkite were No. 1 in viewership when it came to news programming.

News vs. Business

Cronkite knew that TV news was highly vulnerable to the economic whims of the network bosses. Entertainment programming had hit its stride and was making buckets of money for CBS. So it was an open question as to how much money and airtime would be allotted to news.

The legendary newsman put it this way once:

"I visualize the TV industry as a huge building dedicated to the business of entertainment. Journalism is an attached annex next door. In that door between them is a huge vacuum that runs 24 hours a day, threatening to suck into the larger building, anyone who comes too close."

A momentary truce

But when Kennedy was shot in Dallas, in-house battles like that paused. The network bosses scrubbed most of its entertainment programming in the days following the assassination, and the news took center stage. Even television commercials were scaled way back until after the Kennedy funeral.

We were all glued to our TV sets; most of us watching CBS, Cronkite, and some of the best reporters in the world do their job. Among them were names that came to be legends including Dan Rather, Charles Collingwood, Roger Mudd, and Harry Reasoner.

A revealing study

A survey conducted by the independent research organization NORC at the University of Chicago shows how *much* we were watching.

The survey asked Americans how much time they spent listening to radio or watching television while special coverage aired in the days after the event. And the numbers were very large and remarkably consistent. On each of the four days from Nov. 22 through Nov. 25, between 72% and 75% of respondents said they tuned in for a minimum of five hours of coverage. And more than 40% reported watching or listening to at least nine hours of special television and radio programming each day.

"The impact of the trauma—and perhaps of absorbing all that coverage—was also seen clearly in the NORC survey results," the Pew Foundation wrote. "In the wake of the Kennedy shooting, 68% of respondents reported feeling very nervous and tense, 48% had trouble getting sleep and 43% said they didn't feel like eating."

The nation's living room

Looking back, it was as if 180 million Americans were gathered in the family room to hear our favorite "Uncle Walter" announce that one of our most beloved relatives had just died. The family may have had different opinions about JFK's policies, but the man himself was loved. So full of ideals, so charismatic, so young to die.

In my WPI presentation, I noted what Roger Mudd had said in reflecting on the role TV played in Americans' coming to grips with the assassination:

"At that moment there began something which could only happen in the age of TV. As a nation we were able to live out our grief in concert and, at the same time, begin the tough business of picking up the pieces. Moreover, we were able to prepare ourselves for the new order of things. At the end of four days, we were to know the new president intimately, who he was, where he came from and, most important of all, how he behaved in a time of extreme stress."

Unity or Divisiveness?

Today we usually don't think of the news media as a unifier. Quite the contrary, we know that the plethora of outlets aids our divisiveness. The common pool of information that we had in 1963 has morphed into a maelstrom of countless competing news and opinion sites. And the *common* commitment among news outlets to nonpartisan, factual reporting is just not there.

Taking its place in so many outlets is pure, unvarnished ideology.

Disappearing facts

So, would the news media have the same impact today, were such a national tragedy to occur again? As a journalist, I know some legitimate news outlets would try their best to make that happen by delivering solid, fact-anchored reporting.

But I also know so many outlets — and a multitude of tweets and Facebook posts — would find ways of distorting or ignoring the facts out of self-interest for their ideology and/or wallets.

In the end, I fear the result would probably not be unity, but more division. Hopefully, we won't have to test that grim prediction.

38

The Big Sister Factor

C.J. and me, circa 1963.
Hazel M. Willis

Family relationships can be complicated, and we all know that. I have to say, however, that the easiest one for me has been my relationship with my big sister, C.J. (short for Cecelia Jane).

When my book of life is written, C.J. will be a key character in it and — perhaps — the single most significant reason for the surprisingly positive way I seem to have turned out.

A Guiding Light

She has been my true north star throughout life since my toddler days in Columbus, Ohio, when she was chasing me around the yard trying to plant sloppy kisses on me. Her life's work, dedication, and caring spirit speak for themselves, and she has always been a great adviser to me in life.

196

C.J. was a Midwest City High School senior when I was a sophomore in Oklahoma, and she was much more popular than I was in school. For the first year, I seemed to walk in her shadow and didn't mind a bit.

The Pathfinder

In her senior year, she was voted a runner-up in the annual Miss MCHS Pageant. When she graduated in 1962, she went on to the University of Oklahoma and became a dorm counselor (now called resident advisor) in Cate Center, then the school's women's dorm complex.

Had it not been for C.J., my life would have taken a different trajectory. I was planning on joining the Navy right after high school, then considered going to Oklahoma State University. I even applied and was accepted to OSU.

It looked like the Navy was going to win out over college, though, as I entered my last semester of Midwest City High School. That's when C.J. took me out to dinner one night, reminded me she *was a girls dorm counselor at OU,* and convinced me she could introduce me to *all* of those young women if I liked.

Whatever works

She knew of my interest in the opposite sex, felt that might be the button to punch, and it was. So, in many ways, I went to college because of my big sister and having an inside track to meet OU girls who didn't want to get sideways with their dorm counselor.

As my mom would later comment, "Hey, great. Whatever works!"

But C.J.'s professional contribution to the world was much greater than getting her brother into college. In her own right, she returned to Midwest City to teach speech, drama, and English at Jarman and later at Choctaw High School.

She also served several churches as a pastor's wife and musical accompanist over a half-century. She wound up the last 15 years of her career co-founding a highly successful Midwest City home school, called ECHO, and serving as its chief administrator for many years.

In Mom's footsteps

When I think of her doing that, I am reminded of our mother, who did a similar thing back in 1950 when she began Jack & Jill Preschool, the first curriculum-driven preschool in this young, 8-year-old town.

Both Mom's and C.J.'s school programs benefitted Midwest City school children, and they did so 50 years apart.

When I think of my relationship with C.J., though, I think mostly about her being my main go-to person, other than my wife Annie, when I just need a good friend who will listen and support me. She's done this plenty of times, even when she must have thought I was crazy.

She hasn't always let me off the hook when my ideas have been wrong, but she has always let me know she loves me and is there for me. And I think, in knowing that, I have felt more like getting myself back on the right course.

The love and respect I feel for my sister have proven to be strong motivators to straighten myself out in life.

Sometimes a guy just needs his big sister.

The ubiquitous ethernet cord of the dial-up age of computers
Michael Schwarzenberger/Pixabay

39

The Song(?) Remembers When

Years ago, while teaching in Memphis, I found myself a bachelor for the first time in two decades, and I would long for the past when I had a partner in life. Then I'd hear a song that struck the right chord with my loneliness, and my mind would go back to the days of love.

That year, the country singer Trisha Yearwood had a hit song about this phenomenon, it's at the following link, and it was called, *The Song Remembers When*.

We all know that simply hearing an old song can transport us back in time. Perhaps we remember those times as happier ones, because the angst is removed from them. We know how things turned out, and we know we survived.

And then there's *noise*

But all noises and all sounds do not make songs, yet still they carry us back in time. And, like songs, not always to happier times.

If you slept through the dial-up phase of Internet access technology, you will not know the loud grating and agonizingly slow sound of your computer trying to connect to the Web . If you waited to awake in the age of Wi-Fi, you're one of the lucky ones. For the rest of us, the dial-up sound is very similar to R2D2 being bashed about by an angry Stormtrooper, and it is impossible to forget.

The blessed ethernet cord delivered that hellish sound and played it right into your Sony headset every time you went online.

The cord had to be plugged into a phone jack, or the thing that was never close to where your computer was. Even if it was, you sometimes wanted more privacy like when you wanted to order that expensive guitar without your spouse seeing you do it.

The hallway cord

So, to achieve that solitude, you excused yourself from her company, said you had to talk business with your boss, and you didn't want to disturb her *Jeopardy* viewing.

Then you unhooked the short ethernet cord from the phone jack, replaced it with a 40-foot python from your computer bag, uncoiled it down the hallway into your bedroom, and shut the door.

You had your Nirvana and of course your loving wife didn't suspect a thing.

There, in the peaceful privacy of your bedroom, you dialed up the Internet connection, using one of the numbers the Internet provider gave you. And then, in a couple seconds, your solitude was blasted apart by the agonizing wailing and sputtering of R2D2 being kicked about in a metallic warehouse.

It wasn't just the *sound* that was so annoying. Making the noise even more infuriating was the *time* it could take to actually make the connection to the Net, because a hoard of other *netziens* in your area were logging on, and your cable was limited in capacity.

Waiting for Godot

So you waited. And waited. And waited.

As you did your waiting, you sometimes recalled your childhood days of the old telephone party lines. You remembered waiting for Clara to finish telling Ophelia about how *huge* her spring cucumbers were before she hung up. At last you had your person-to-person privacy.

Back to the current moment, when finally you broke through to your browser, you remember it being one of the happiest times of the evening. You began browsing the online catalogue of guitars and found the one you wanted about a half-hour later.

You are not alone

You were ready to place your order when two things happened in sudden sequence. First came the loud *yelp!* from the hallway, and then your computer screen went black.

Opening the door, you glimpsed the tail of your dog running for her life around the corner into the living room. Then you looked down at the ethernet cord and found you now had *two* cords. The chewed ends of this electrical line were still smoldering, and you shed no tears over your dog. Of course, he was just fine.

From that night forward, you have defined *progress* as the day Wi-Fi was invented. But you're still trying to get that ugly dial-up song out of your head.

40

Washday Miracle in Stillwater

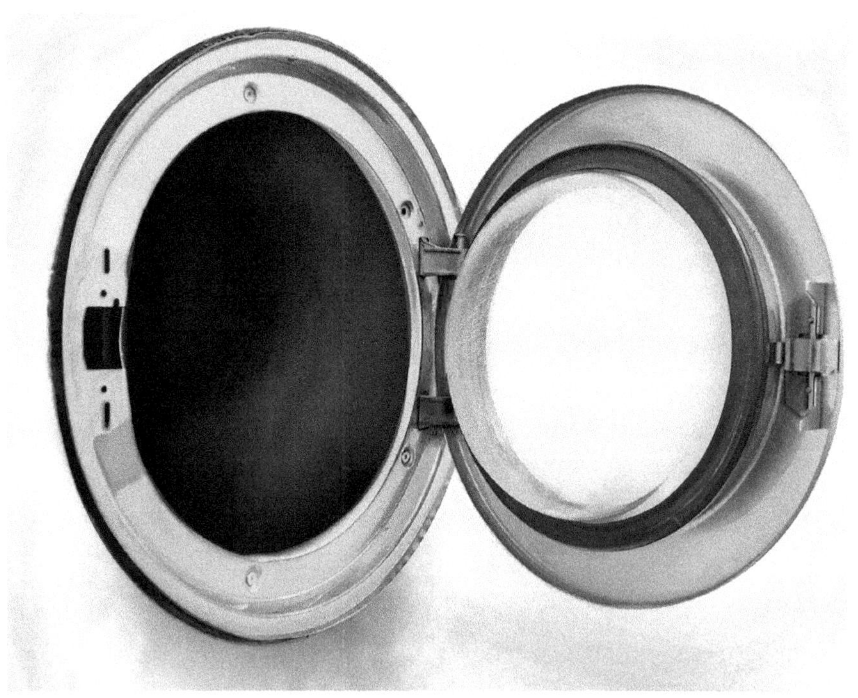

It looks harmless enough, but it may not be.

E ver since November 1, 1964, I have been reluctant to stick my hand in a washer or dryer to retrieve clothing. Alas, it is a fear

I've had to overcome because repeatedly buying new socks and under-wear was clearly not a sustainable practice.

My hesitation to hang out in laundry rooms began on that date 59 years ago when I heard the news about Bob Swaffar, a sophomore bas-ketball player at nearby Oklahoma State University. It was on that Tuesday night when Swaffar reached into an industrial dryer in the laundry room of Lewis Field in Stillwater, Oklahoma. He was pulling out an old pair of Levi's.

The *other* green monster

The OSU athletes had dubbed the dryer "the green monster" be-cause it was so huge and powerful. Essentially it was meant to dry an entire team's worth of uniforms at once. It dried mostly by sucking water out of the clothing as it was spinning. Something like a megasize swimming trunk water extractor that you find in pool locker rooms.

On this Tuesday night, however, it extracted more than water. The green monster extracted Bob Swaffar's right arm just below the shoul-der.

The guy who decided at the last minute to play basketball at OSU,rather than go to Princeton, hit the floor fully conscious, but in a state of shock as blood spewed from his shoulder like a water foun-tain. Fortunately, his teammates were close by and rushed in to help him, aghast at the scene in front of them. Swafford was doubled over on the floor, and his arm was still in the dryer, covered in blood.

A fortunate irony

Ironically, teammate Gary Hassman (who would go on himself to become a doctor) had just been reading about a doctor in Boston who performed the first successful reattachment of a human limb, some-thing which was new in the early 1960s. He had read that the severed arm was put on ice immediately after his patient had lost it, and that helped save it allow to become functioning once again.

Hassman was standing nearby and was pelted with fragments of bone and blood. He turned and saw the sight and yelled for one of his teammates to "Grab the arm and put it on ice!" That is what Jimmy

Tom Watson did, although there was no ice around so he filled a tub with cold water and placed the arm in it.

Then he and teammate Lester Berryhill turned to comfort Swaffar who was still on the floor and dazed. His teammates grabbed towels and began wrapping them tightly around the open wound in Swaffar shoulder. Then one of them called for an ambulance.

The question

"What, what happened?" asked Swaffar.

"Nothing, Bob," Berryhill whispered. "You just hurt your arm." In truth, no one really knows how it happened. There was a foot pedal on the dryer to stop its spinning, but did anyone actually step on it?

The ambulance arrived, and Swaffar was rushed to University Hospital. It was there that doctors called an Oklahoma City physician, Dr. Rainey Williams, who had studied the Boston arm reattachment surgery, and was doing his own experimentations on animals. Williams immediately drove the hour-long trip to Stillwater to perform the revolutionary surgery on Swaffar, having gotten permission from the patient to do so.

The outcome

"I think it was successful," Dr. Williams told Swaffar's parents after the operation. It was only the third successful arm reattachment ever performed in the United States.

Swaffar's basketball career was over, but he emerged with a partially functioning arm and hand, went on to become president of the student senate, graduate with a math degree in 1967, and then received Masters degrees in architecture and computer science from the University of Texas at Austin.

A successful career

He served a year in the Peace Corps and was hired in the early 1990s by UT to direct the computer lab for its School of Architecture and married a professor of German there. Swaffar retired in 2003 and devoted himself to the artform of making clay pottery which he had pursued much of his life. Today he is a ceramic artist living in Austin and exhibiting his work in shows and festivals like the Texas Clay Festival.

In 1994, Swaffar told reporter Berry Trammel, he owes his life to his teammates and that he is glad he decided to let Dr. Williams try the experimental arm reattachment surgery.

A "huge difference"

"[Having the arm] made a huge difference as far as my confidence and the way I functioned in life," he told Trammel. "To be an amputee would be very difficult compared to the situation I have."

He added that he's learned to overcome both the still-occurring nerve pain and the inconvenience of not having two completely functional hands. He compares the use of his arm to the use that the late Sen. Bob Dole had of his war-damaged arm.

Most of those who have seen and bought his pottery don't even know the artist's laundry room story of 1964. And they would be amazed that such fine artwork could be turned out by a man who lost his arm. And then found it again.

(Note: Although I was a high school senior in Oklahoma when this 1964 accident happened and I remember it clearly, much of this story is based on the facts that my former colleague, Tulsa World reporter Berry Trammel, gathered and reported on extensively.)

41

A Distant Trumpet

Some people find comfort in the rhythm of their own song.
Stocksnap/Pixabay

A friend of mine got lost on his way to the stars. He may simply have been born into the wrong galaxy, because I doubt he has felt comfortable in this one, save for short periods of his life.

Part of the reason for this is Jonathan G. Embrey himself; the unique way he was made, and the way he reacted to this world into which he was born. Still, in my early years, Jonathan was an inspiration to me and the friend with whom I felt comfortable.

But part of Jonathan's later troubled life was a result of PTSD during the Vietnam Era when the military draft robbed so many young American men of their lives and sent many others into fighting personal wars with depression and guilt. That came to be called Post Traumatic Stress Disorder. And that is a condition a person must live with to fully understand how debilitating it can be.

Often, I wonder if we really give full credit to those who choose to live with PTSD and fight it rather than make a choice to end their lives.

Vietnam and the Cold War Era of the 1960s and 70s gave us plenty of men who faced these decisions.

Jonathan is one of the brave fighters of this dreaded syndrome, and I am proud of him for it. I am also saddened he has had to deal with it. But I love remembering the friend I knew when I was younger.

We met in Junior High School while he still lived in my town, of Midwest City. We bonded soon and then his parents became wealthy and moved to a larger place in Oklahoma City where he attended Northwest Classen High School.

So, Jonathan and I attended different high schools, but we still saw each other a lot, especially when we both got cars after we turned 16. After graduating from our high schools, we both went to the same college and continued our friendship there.

But we lost track of each other when we pursued our own career and life paths following college and graduate school. The last time I saw Jonathan was in the fall of 1978 in Kansas City. I was starting a Ph.D. program at the University of Missouri in Columbia, and Jonathan had just finished his graduate work in architecture at the University of Kansas and was starting his career with an architectural firm in Kansas City.

It had been 10 years since we graduated with our BA degrees from college. He enlisted in the military rather than wait to be drafted, then went on to grad school. I became a working journalist and then began preparing to transition into college teaching.

One weekend in November 1978, I needed a break from my studies, located Jonathan's phone number, called him, and we set up a meeting at his new home. Kansas City was only a couple hours away from me, and we had an enjoyable weekend reunion. Still, I could tell Jonathan was conflicted about something, maybe down deep, and he seemed to be trying too hard to act as if he were okay.

When we parted company and I went back to Missouri, we wished each other well and said of course we'd stay in touch. And, of course, we didn't. Our lives got busy, Jonathan moved to another state and job, and that was the last we saw each other. Ever.

When I think of him, which I often do, I remember a guy who liked to live by the beat of his own music. He was a trumpet master, even at a young age, and I think he felt most comfortable playing while alone, although he was often asked to perform for others. I understood his desire for solitude, because that's how I was when playing my guitar. I was a little too uncomfortable playing in front of others, and I think Jonathan was, too. Yet Jonathan still became known as one of the best young trumpeters in the state.

And was this guy ever intelligent! Jonathan was sharper than a carpet tack when it came to knowledge about nearly any subject I could think of. Our bonding in school was unusual, given I kept myself treading a sea (or "C") of academic mediocrity, while he was commanding a metaphorical battleship of intelligence.

When you asked Jonathan a weighty question, you could almost hear the gears start grinding in his head as he scrolled for the correct, clear, and specific answer. As he tilted his head back slightly and squinted his eyes, he often would do this little dance with his hands, closing them into fists and then extending his two opposing index fingers as they stared at each other a couple inches apart and rotated in opposite circles. While this miniature ballet was in motion, his head would bob slightly, side to side, and his tongue would click softly off the roof of his mouth.

"*Tch, tch, tch, tch, tch...*"

Jonathan Embrey was thinking. And you were dead sure the answer that would emerge from all this personal posturing cum stagecraft would be an illuminating one.

"Give me a minute, and I'll get back to you with this," he might say. Then, just a few seconds later, he would deliver his conclusions.

"All right, it lays out like this. To the first part of your question, yes, but with the following qualifications ..." and then he would reel off a clear and convincing response. Whether you agreed with it or not, you were impressed and you knew you'd be no match for him in a rebuttal.

To some, Jonathan was maybe seen as a nerd. Just not your typical nerd, though. More of a cool nerd with an edge.

For one thing, he played that mean horn and would often wear this little black French beret and horizontally striped t-shirt when he played. Sort of looked like a refugee from Mutiny on the Bounty or a Gilbert and Sullivan musical.

Most probably he was just trying to evoke the model of a beatnik. The late 1950s and early 1960s were, after all, their era. Typified by television's Maynard G. Krebs of Dobie Gillis fame.

In actual appearance, Jonathan was not traditional movie star material but did have an X Factor. Standing about 5'8", of average frame and body, sporting short, cropped curly brown hair, fighting a bout with high school acne. But he always dressed cool. Cool by 1964 standards, that is. Button-down collar, the right pants and right shoes, not bad really.

If he were to pick a TV character Jonathan would like to be compared to, it would be Patrick McGoohan of the 1967 futuristic series, *The Prisoner,* which became a cult favorite with viewers and with Jonathan. The show featured a former British spy known only as Number Six who was struggling to escape what appeared to be a perfect village, except that it favored control and conformity over individual free will. Each week Number Six would try to escape; each week he would fail.

I can almost see the McGoohan similarity in terms of looks but certainly in terms of the fix Jonathan found himself in. He didn't warm up to either control or conformity any more than Number Six did.

Still, if I were to pick a character he resembled more, I'd pick someone like Richard Dreyfus' character Elliot Garfield in Neil Simon's 1977's film comedy *The Goodbye Girl*. One trait Jonathan and Elliot had in common is their biting wit, and Jonathan often showed that trait, as per this memory:

It came when I attended a performance he gave at his high school across Oklahoma City from mine. While playing a trumpet solo before a packed house in the auditorium, something struck Jonathan as funny, and he flat busted out laughing, right into his horn. He blew the Harmon mute right out the end of the trumpet, and it went clacking across the wooden stage.

The audience fell silent. Undaunted, Jonathan walked across the stage, picked up the mute, stuffed it back into his horn, and turned to face his audience. With a poker-face look and hunched shoulders that bespoke, "I'd rather be in Philadelphia," he announced to the audience, "And now, for my *next* trick ..." Then he put the trumpet back to his lips and belted out a wonderful jazz number that had us all standing and applauding.

Intelligence and wit. That was Jonathan. And they were the two qualities that kept him such an interesting person to me. Overall, he was just a nice guy that did his own thing and gave me space to do mine.

Had *The West Wing* been made back in the 60s, he could have played the Bradley Whitford role of Josh Lyman, although a more neurotic Lyman, uncomfortable around his fellow workers and especially so at parties.

But Jonathan was a multitasker, even before computers, and his pragmatic nature would have acquitted him well in any profession he wanted. The challenge he faced was conforming to others' social expectations. He seemed to live largely solo, on his own terms, allowing his thoughts, dreams and fantasies to offer him comfort.

Growing up, Jonathan seemed an unlikely candidate for one who preferred privacy over socializing. His folks became popular and wealthy in Oklahoma City, and they enjoyed throwing parties for friends at their large home.

But, during those parties, Jonathan would usually be in his room, either playing or listening to music and thinking his own thoughts. Think of the Dustin Hoffman character Ben in the 1967 film, *The Graduate*. Remember when Ben's folks coaxed him out of his room at the graduation party, they threw for him?

Ben came, but he came in his new SCUBA gear and immediately jumped into the deep end of the pool and stayed there, looking up at the watery images of the guests on the pool deck. He liked it better down on the bottom.

Despite what seemed his quirkiness, my friend Jonathan kept advancing in life, at least for two more decades after high school, because it simply wasn't in him not to. He graduated summa cum laude from college, performed his required military service, graduated from a top school of architecture and worked for several years in that profession in another state. The only reason I know this, however, is because his mother and mine attended church together and chatted occasionally.

But when my mother died, the news reports of Jonathan came to an end.

Years passed, my life took its own twists and turns, and Jonathan Embrey faded from memory except for momentary flashbacks to our young years together.

Then, one day in 2006 when I was back in Oklahoma visiting my parents, I decided to at least make an effort to find him and see how he was doing. I asked mutual friends about Jonathan, but they had not seen or heard from him either. I finally discovered by accident that he had bought a place in Oklahoma City.

I am not built to intrude into other people's lives (which I realize is a strange thing for a journalist to say), and I was hesitant about giving Jonathan a call. But I did, anyway. The call I made that day was a brief one and left an eerie, sad feeling.

The phone rang several times before being answered.

The voice sounded older than I expected, it sounded tired, and it sounded odd, but still it was him. I continued cautiously, not presuming it actually was Jonathan.

"Hi. This is Jim Willis, and I'm trying to locate Jonathan Embrey," I said. Something in his voice made me approach it this way, even though I was pretty sure it was him. Maybe give him an out if he didn't want to talk? Not sure.

A pause followed, and then an emphatic, *"Not here."*

No doubt now: It was his voice, and it was his style. Back in college he often dropped the subject out of short responses as in...

"Looks like it."

Or

"Think not."

"Not here," fit his pattern and after three decades since I'd

last heard it, the voice was Jonathan. The uncomfortable feeling of invading a person's privacy, which had swept over me while I dialed his number, became even more pronounced now. Maybe I was just projecting what I'd feel if I were trying to live life like a recluse, but it seemed plausible. This smart and ambitious guy who had come back home for whatever reason, the guy who had avoided forty years of reunions at his school like they were rattlesnakes, the guy who had disappeared from the face of the earth, was letting me know he did not want to be found.

"Not here."

It rang in my ears and reverberated as if bouncing off the canyon walls back home in California's San Gabriel Valley. But why didn't he want to be found?

Or was it just that he didn't, for some reason, want to be found by me? Could it be Jonathan wasn't up to swapping life stories with a guy who he hadn't seen in a couple decades? A guy who had struggled just to make his grades, way back when, while Jonathan was acing the toughest major the university had to offer? And that to be followed a few years later by his graduating from one of the country's top architecture schools?

I know I tend to let my imagination run wild sometimes, but all I had to go on here was my memory of Jonathan himself, and a gut feeling about what had happened.

I sensed something traumatic happened in his life. A lot of men our age were fighting emotional battles resulting from the Vietnam Era when PTSD ran rampant among young soldiers. That was certainly true in Vietnam, but also for those serving along the Berlin Wall in Germany. They were scary times to be a soldier or government agent.

Was that Jonathan's case? Was that why I heard, *"Not here."*?

Not, "He's not in, but can I take your number, and I'll have him give you a call when he returns?"

Not, "He's stepped out for a couple hours but will be back."

Not, "He will be sorry to have missed your call."

Just, *"Not here."*

Period. End of conversation. End of story. Or at least, that's what the voice wanted. I couldn't help but think, however, that *"Not here"* also spoke at a deeper level to that fact that the Jonathan Embrey I had known was, in fact, not there. I couldn't help but wonder why.

Nevertheless, I decided instantly not to press the matter. Not to say into the receiver, "Come on Jonathan, I know that's you. What's up, man?" Maybe, if it had only been a year since we last spoke, but not these many years. I just let it go in the interest of his privacy, at least for the moment.

"Okay, sorry for the interruption," I said, as if I didn't know whom I was talking to.

There were no goodbyes before he hung up. Just the click of the receiver.

Whether I was right or wrong, I could feel I just wasn't wanted or needed in Jonathan's life this night.

Still, here he was. I knew that now. All it would take would be driving a half-hour into Oklahoma City and knocking on his door.

Yet, somehow, that seemed a door too far.

There is an epilogue to this story. Ten years later, about 2016, I had moved to Kentucky and one day I got an e-mail from Jonathan congratulating me on a book of mine he had seen. It had to do with life behind the Iron Curtain in East Germany. He told me had served his military duty in West Germany as an intelligence specialist, his life had been in danger, and he did develop PTSD. It was still troubling him, more than a little, all these years later.

An indication of that? This parting statement he wrote after telling me of his lingering apprehensions:

"On that happy note," my friend wrote. "I think I'll go see if all pistols have been cleaned lately!"

But the good news was that Jonathan had been doing a lot of writing on his own Cold War Era experiences as an intelligence agent. I told him it was my turn to be impressed, thanked him for his service, and said I hoped he was finding peace in his new writings. He was always such a great researcher.

He told me his life plans took a punch in the gut when the architectural firm he worked for had downsized at the height of his career. By then, he was past 50, the nation was in a recession, and he decided to return to Oklahoma and see what life would bring.

He responded, "I've gotten used to my life, living alone, although I admit to some bitterness about what's been tossed my way. The PTSD from my military days still haunts me, and let's just say the Veterans Administration could have been more helpful in my recovery."

And then he switched gears and added this sad statement: I'm afraid I was a lousy friend to you, though, Jim."

I replied, "Jonathan, on the contrary, you were a good friend. I consider you that still. You meant a lot to me growing up. You made me see the sense in learning, and you were an inspiration."

We said we'd stay in touch, but we haven't, save for a couple emails. I can't really say why, although I don't get back to Oklahoma much now.

I do know I feel better about the mystery of Jonathan Embrey being solved. But I wished my instincts, now twenty years ago, had been wrong about the PTSD. They weren't.

I feel a little better just knowing he is okay in living life the solitary way he's chosen. Or has it been chosen for him? I know it's hard for him. He is one of a countless number of military veterans whose service to their country in times of conflict wound up robbing them of the joy and the promising futures they would have had, were it not for the PTSD.

I will always wish Jonathan happiness, elusive though it's been for him.

You meant a lot to me, pal, and I'll always remember you as a friend and a hero.

Midnight at the dawn of the Millennium, I've got Mail
Pixabay

42

Cupid on the Keys

As the last days of the year 1999 counted down to the 21st Century, we were all wondering how this landmark New Year's Eve would play out. The big question was what might happen to our personal computers and the data they carried?

Would they become high-tech pumpkins?

Y2K issue

This fear that settled over the world had some merit to it, and it was called the "Y2K Problem." The concern was of potential computer errors related to the formatting and storage of calendar data for dates in and after the year 2000.

Many computer programs represented four-digit years with only the final two digits, making the year 2000 indistinguishable from 1900. Computer systems' inability to distinguish data correctly had the potential to bring down worldwide infrastructures for industries ranging from banking to air travel. In the case of me and my university colleagues, all our stored research and class notes were at stake.

What might happen to all that data? Would the changeover to the 2000s scramble our stored data? Make it inaccessible? Would there be a loud pop at midnight coming from inside our desktops, followed by a plume of smoke coming out the ventilator slits?

All of the above? None of the above?

Faculty on guard

At the University of Memphis, we faculty were advised to back up computer data and monitor our computers on the night of Dec. 31, looking for signs of damage caused by the sweep of the clock's minute hand past midnight 2000.

Since I was single and my love life was drowning in the tank, I had no plans on New Year's Eve, so I spent the night in my office — probably the only one in my building to do so — and babysat my desktop Mac. Happily, the night passed safely for it and my data.

No smoke

I breathed a sigh of relief when the clock struck 12 and my computer failed to explode. Indeed, it just sat there and looked at me like I was an idiot for camping out in my office instead of going out and partying.

What I didn't know was that Cupid was right there with me. At 12:05 a.m., he reached over and flipped up my AOL flag alerting me that, *"You've got mail!"*

Who, I wondered, would be writing me just after midnight on New Year's Eve? Could there be someone else as foolish as me at the university who was nursing their own computer in their office and saw the light from mine through the window?

I clicked the message open and was surprised to find a mystery woman had written me, telling me she loves to bake chocolate chip cookies and believes them to be the best in the country. Quickly I realized she was responding to my "must love dogs" post on the *One and Only* dating site, wherein I had mentioned I love chocolate chip cookies.

A surprise date

Wow, I thought. Looks like I have a date on New Year's Eve after all! Her name was Anne, she lived one state over, in Kentucky, and she had found my profile interesting enough to write and say hi.

She liked the fact I was a journalist and an educator, she joked about my references to my world travel and to the fact I actually had an Indiana Jones snap-brim fedora hat. She said any man who seemed that rugged, had a Ph.D, and yet still had a soft spot for chocolate chip cookies must be okay.

Anne did not post a profile picture, which usually lessens the chance for a response on dating sites. But she seemed so sweet and clever that I wasted no time in responding.

"So, your bakery must be open all night," I wrote. "Since I live in Memphis, it's unlikely I can swing by to sample your cookies, but maybe we can talk awhile online, anyway. Are you up for that?"

Taking it slow

So, yeah, we did talk more. A lot more. And, for the first time in a long time, I was actually thinking something was going right in my life; something which I absolutely did not deserve. But I resolved I would gladly take it, anyway.

A couple days later she did send me her photo, and she was as pretty as her online personality predicted she would be. The photo showed her dancing with her father (who bore a striking resemblance to Jimmy Carter) at her daughter Mollye's wedding. She had a smile that brightened up the dance floor, and I predicted – correctly, as it turned out – that Anne and I would be talking a lot more.

A song in her heart

She told me she was a musician, with degrees from the University of Kentucky, and that she was performing with her local community theater and was about to play the role of Miss Hannigan in *Annie* (obviously against type for such a pretty actress). She was recently divorced and had three daughters.

I wasted no time in responding and telling her about my two sons.

The month of January passed, and I felt a new breeze blowing through my daily life. I was buoyed by the possibility that Anne represented. I was actually happy for a change.

Reading the tea leaves

About a month into our online exchanges, Anne and I felt confident enough to set up an in-person Kentucky meeting in Lexington, not far from her home in Winchester. We agreed to meet at a wonderful bookstore called Joseph Beth which had a pleasant café' on its first floor.

We set the meeting for the night of Feb. 14. Valentine's Day seemed appropriate. I arrived about 6 p.m., and Anne was already there. I had written her I'd be wearing a burnt orange barn coat, and when she spotted me, she came to the front of the café to greet me, holding out her hand. We shook and she took me back to our table.

I cannot remember what we ate, but I will always remember feeling so comfortable talking with her. She spoke of her daughters, her community theater work, and of what it was like growing up in Kentucky. She was a very young-looking 47 and I was surprised to find her oldest daughter had already graduated from college.

She was very self-possessed, independent, and secure in her womanhood. She was also straightforward and, she had already let me know in an email what she would like the ground rules to be of our face-to-face meeting.

"Jim," she had written, "I look forward to meeting you in person but, in case we don't feel a connection, let's have an understanding that we chalk our meeting up to a nice dinner conversation and then go our own ways in life."

No Jolene

Wow! I thought, as the relief flowed through me. This is not going to be another Nashville experience with a desperate woman we'll call Jolene who tried (unsuccessfully) to trap me in her guest bedroom overnight by sleeping on the floor on the other side of the door I had locked firmly. But that's another story.

This woman Anne does just fine on her own, I thought. Better than I'd been doing myself over the past four years in trying to pick up the pieces of a shattered dream.

Closing time

We talked about three hours straight, and the cafe' was ready to close up. So, we each paid our own check (another of her ground rules) and went into the lobby of the connected Hilton hotel where I was spending the night.

Anne and me on our 20th anniversary.

Our new relationship was off to a good start. I had learned years ago about the relative value of being able to converse easily and deeply with a very interesting and intelligent woman.

After another hour of talking, we said our goodbyes as I walked her to her car out in the parking lot, allowing ourselves to at least embrace in a good-night hug at her car. But she did invite me over to her home in nearby Winchester for breakfast the next morning. I readily accepted, she got into her car and I waved goodbye and walked back to my hotel.

This much I knew

As I reflected later on the evening, I realized two things: first, I liked Anne very much, and second, that while the idea of taking things slow was different for me, it was best if we did it that way.

Neither of us was sure we'd found the one we'd been looking for, but we did sense that this was a promising relationship and we wanted to see each other again.

So that's what we did. Again and again and again. Today, in fact, we've been seeing each other daily for a quarter century as husband and wife.

She has come to my rescue, and I've been able to help her out with her graduate education. She holds two master's degrees from Azusa Pacific University where I taught for many years, and she received greatly reduced tuition prices as part of my benefits package at the school.

Anne calls us pioneers from the early days of digital dating. We were in the first wave of couples who found each other online, for sure. Back when it wasn't so easy to find independent confirmation that the guy or girl you met, was really who they said they were. So it was a bit daring then. But it worked out great for us.

So, if she calls me her fellow pioneer, I just call her my *Millennial Woman*. We were married in the year 2000.

Anything will work as a pillow for Blue, even her sister Bogan.
Anne Willis

43

The Furry Feud

*W*hen *the weather turns cold*
and the skies turn gray
The indoors becomes our outdoors
and our minds give way.

Don't bother Googling that ditty, because you won't find it. But it does fit Anne and me and the trouble we often get into around this time of year. It's when we become bored, and it's the kind of boredom that could lead to a family feud, were it not for two saving graces:

1. We both love animals. (but we disagree on how many is enough)

2. Anne has a wonderful sense of humor (but nothing. It has probably saved us from divorce).

As I scroll back in time, through the three-month span of December through February, I realize these are the months that so many of our 25 dogs and 5 cats have come into our lives over our 22+ years of marriage.

During these months, Anne and I choose to beat those winter blues by combing through the websites for discarded pets, finding the most doe-eyed of the bunch, then going and adopting them.

Anne is usually the troublemaker who gets the ball rolling. But nearly always, once the new animal has won my heart, I'm glad she is, and does.

Anne and I met online, back on New Year's Eve 1999, and our coming together gave new meaning to the oft-stated dating post requirement, "Must love dogs." Still, during my times of protest over adding yet another dog, there is a tinge of tension around our place. It lasts until I see the error of my ways in doubting Anne's sanity. It's hard to stay angry with a woman who knows how to make you laugh.

It's not that Anne doesn't know that the last thing we need is another dog or cat. It's not like I've lost track of the number of sane moments when she has pleaded with me, "Jim, if I ever start talking about getting another dog, please just shoot me. OK?!"

"Although I've never seriously thought about doing that, there have been times when I pondered padlocking the doors of our home and melting down the key.

That said, the latest three adoptees, our foxhound George, our greyhound Yoyo, and our English Setter Blue, have proven to be worthy successors to their long line of ancestors who have since crossed the famed rainbow bridge.

Those dearly departed were dogs like Margie and Charlie, the two Golden Retrievers who still claim large pieces of our hearts.

Then there was Maggie, who caused a vacuous vet tech to become vexed when we boarded both Maggie and her sister (of the same name but different breed) at the same time.

"But how will we tell them apart?" she actually asked. "I mean, they *do* have the same name!"

We're talking about a reddish Chow and a very black Lab here.

Feeling sorry for her, we lowered the vet tech's stress level by color-coding the two Maggie names: Red Maggie and Black Maggie.

"Oh, thank you!" the grateful young woman gushed, but added, "We'll just make sure by tying different colored ribbons on their collars."

Right. Whatever.

Then there was Hazel, the rescued cat who warmed up to us more like a dog would, and who helped us raise every pup brought home during her lifetime. Hazel is the cat who made me rethink my skepticism about felines. She was one cool cat.

So these three latest canine additions have kept the great-dog tradition alive in our home.

The greyhound came to us as a young retiree from the track in Tijuana. Before she reached the age of 2, she had already convinced her owners she was pursuing the wrong career. After scanning her racing record and seeing the number of times she was marked as "DNF" (did not finish), we knew we had to call this lovable dog, Yoyo. I mean, she would just stop flat in mid-race and return to the starting gate.

As for George, he has the best eye contact of any dog I've ever had. So many times have we stared into each other's eyes, I could swear we are talking to each other and understand each other perfectly.

Blue is the latest boarder at Willis Farms and, quite possibly, the zaniest and neediest dog I've ever met. Check that; I think I just met a new winner for those prizes. But Blue is a dog who would just lay down and die if she didn't have a family showing her unbounded affection, 24/7. She is absolutely wonderful.

All three are perfect examples of how our boredom in the early winter months has resulted in making ours an even happier home, in addition to helping boost the value of Ralston-Purina on the New York Stock Exchange.

Still every time I head over to Rural King, as I'm doing tomorrow, to pick up another 48-pound bag of dog food and a giant box of 120 Greenies to see us through next week, I wonder if this is what a septuagenarian couple really should be doing.

I think about times like last month when I was recovering from knee surgery, yet still taking the three dogs for daily walks, all at the same time. On this particular day, Yoyo the greyhound spotted a rabbit dashing across the street. Perhaps remembering what she was bred for, she took off after it. Unfortunately, this happened at the moment I was in mid-stride, stepping off the curb into the street. Yoyo (followed by George and Blue) bolted, my leg (the bad one) came down hard on the street, andmy recovery was set back a couple weeks.

In the back of my mind was Anne's oft-uttered plea: "Jim, if I ever start talking about getting another dog, please just shoot me!"

"Nah," I said to myself. "Wouldn't do any good." The word has long since gone out about us to all dogs and cats in need of rescue: "Check in with these two first!"

I know, I know ... this reflection is supposed to be about feuds instead of a lovestruck family of humans and animals, Well, Anne and I are probably a couple months away from our next squabble over dogs and cats.

Then again, maybe not. Anne just told me she has found a site offering Black Friday deals on Golden Retriever puppies. She's got that look in her eyes and, as I'm looking down at Yoyo, she is covering her eyes with a paw.

Just great, she's thinking.

The next weekend has just and we are set to meet a woman from downstate. She's bringing a tiny fuzzy passenger who she is leaving with us.

The eight-week-old's name is Bogan. Anne got her Golden. And remember that new neediest dog prize-winner I mentioned a bit earlier? Along with Blue, she is in our bed snoozing as I write this. It used to be a king size bed, but these days it feels like a twin.

44

My Rubik's Cube of Religion

For many, myself included, religious faith can be like Rubik's Cube.

Pixabay

"Please describe your spiritual journey for us," an employer once asked me.

Although this is a question that would normally seem out of bounds in hiring interviews, I wasn't surprised when the college dean asked it. The reason? I was applying for a faculty leadership position at a faith-based liberal arts college, and I had already been told this question was coming and that it could be a determining factor in my getting hired.

Nevertheless, I must say it was a tough question to answer. For I have always considered my religious faith as something of a metaphorical Rubik's Cube.

I once read, "The Cube can very well represent the intricate and unpredictable journey of existence, with each color on it symbolizing different aspects of life, relationships, and personal growth. Just as every small "cubie" contributes to the overall harmony of the larger puzzle, every experience -- whether joyful or challenging -- shapes the broader tapestry of our life."

"Solving the cube requires patience, perseverance, and methodical problem-solving, reflecting how we as humans navigate setbacks and learn from our mistakes."

Considering myself a fairly bright and sensible guy, however, I had the feeling this was not the kind of convoluted answer my prospective boss might want to hear. After all, this was a college as devoted to its faith stance as to open academic inquiry. That, by the way, is not an easy pair of loyalties for a faculty member to honor if their academic research leads them to conclusions different from parts of the school's faith doctrine.

I knew that the dean just wanted to know if I even *had* a spiritual life and, if so, what did it look like, and how important was it to me? So, I accepted the challenge, offering up the following. Not word for word, but essentially.

My spiritual life began when I started considering faith as something personal instead of institutional. As something inside me instead of something out there. I felt hat was the only way it would have any real meaning for me, apart from being a routine and ritual of going to church.

My pursuit of this began in 1965, when I was 19 and a freshman at the University of Oklahoma.

I was never more open to new inquiries than I was in that first year of college. I felt the world of ideas had just opened up to me. It's the kind of thing that happens to most of us at one time or another.

For example, I've read about the singer Cat Stevens ("Peace Train" and "Moonshadow") and his spiritual discovery. While on holiday in Maraskesh in the 1970s, Stevens was intrigued by the sound of the *adhān,* the Islamic ritual call to prayer, which was explained to him as *"music for God."* Stevens said, "I thought, music for God? I'd never heard that before – I'd heard of music for money, music for fame, music for personal power, but music for God!?

In 1976, the Grammy-winning pop singer, one afternoon found himself in a sudden, tight spot. He was drowning in the Pacific Ocean, while swimming off Malibu. A strong rip tide caught him and began sweeping him out to sea. He called out to God for help and soon felt himself being pulled back to shore by a small wave.

Wanting to give back to this God who had saved him, Stevens pointed himself toward that religion that sang music for God. That led him to the Qur'an and the religion of Islam. He changed his name to Yusuf Islam.

But that was only one key decision he made. The other was to give up his lucrative music career and instead give his life over to international humanitarian causes by promoting and funding the education of poor Middle Eastern children who lived in Europe.

In 2004, Yusuf Islam was ultimately awarded the very first "Man of Peace" prize in Rome at a meeting of Nobel Peace Prize laureates. Former Soviet leader Mikhail Gorbachev, who helped bring down Soviet Communism, awarded him that peace prize in Rome

Though Yusuf chose a religion other than Christianity, the point is he chose to give his life to helping his God and to helping others achieve better futures.

If my two Asian-born sons were seeking a more meaningful faith, I would tell them to first give the man Jesus a long look. Because, at its heart, his is a religion of love and forgiveness. But if they were to find their answers in *another* faith tradition, then I would support them in choosing that one, and hopefully coming alongside of Christianity too. Some people would disagree with me on this, saying I should point out the fallacies of other religions and say Islam is antithetical to the values of Christ. I disagree. I remember the character of Piscene Molitor Patel, the protagonist called Pi, in the novel and film, *The Life of Pi*. What I loved about Pi was that he studied most of the major religions and found something virtuous and helpful in each of Christianity, Islam, Buddhism and Hindu. And, in his life-or-death standoff with the maneating Bengal tiger "Richard Parker" in that small boat at sea, he used lessons learned from each religion to become friends with that tiger. I like to think that what he learned about love from studying Christ was the most helpful lesson in turning his natural enemy into his best friend.

As for my own religious transformation, it came back in 1965 at OU. I felt the need to connect with something larger than myself, and I chose a student house of Christian faith for that connection. It worked for a while, but its effect faded. This particular group was focused on social activism which was important on campuses in the 1960s. It still is.

I did some work with them, but it was not filling the empty spot I felt inside. It was not the hoped-for oasis in my arid life that felt devoid of the felt connection with God that I craved.

So, I continued my search elsewhere, going on into the summer and into my sophomore year of college. One evening I agreed to attend a meeting with a group of students at a fraternity house. Once there, I was curious, because its focus was on establishing a personal relationship with a personal God, rather than just joining the institution of religion in one of the myriad of churches that Oklahoma is known for. It was the first time I really thought of Jesus as a person I could befriend instead of an abstract religious symbol.

God was presented that night as not Somewhere Out There, but Someone Inside Me, and that concept seemed to fit what I was seeking: a way of connecting my life to the God of the Universe. That desire seemed to be shared by everyone else that evening, and that group became my new family on campus for the next three years.

These were loving, educated fellow students, and their influence propelled me into seminary after graduation, just to learn more about my newfound personal Christian faith.

Ever since then, I've tried to keep that faith alive, despite it being built on a narrative that sometimes seems just flat hard for a human to believe and on a connection with a God who sometimes seems distant and outmatched by the challenges I encounter in life.

Several times, I've left the fold and become compromised by wrongheaded habits in pursuit of pleasure.

I have always felt deeply the lyrics from "Come Thou Fount of Every Blessing." Especially so for the verse, *"Prone to wander, Lord I feel it, prone to leave the God I love, here's my heart oh take and seal it, seal it for thy courts above."*

And yet, through all the challenges to that personal faith, through all the ups and downs of that relationship, here I am, still acknowledging that I am a believer, I strive to be a better Christian and -- through that inner force -- a better person, every day.

That pesky doctrinal narrative, although still challenging to me, remains the best documented one of the faith traditions I've studied.

And then there are those inexplicable times when Divine intervention seems the only plausible reason that I escaped successfully from some very tight spots in life. I've conducted searches for other possible causes of those escapes, and I could find none.

One of those moments took place in the late-night hours in a field of northern Mississippi in 1998 when I was coming home to Memphis from a casino where I'd been repeating a self- destructive pattern of gambling.

Overcome with anger and exasperation with myself, I pulled my truck off the country road, turned off the engine and began pounding the wheel and screaming, "I've tried to overcome this and I've asked for help, God! But there's been none, and you've been silent!

Then came my key question: *"What do you want from me?!"*

Instantly, and with great clarity, a response came. It was vocal (at least to me), it was calm, and it was unmistakable. There were only three words, but they were enough on that night and beyond.

The voice said simply, *"I want you."*

I shuddered and felt my eyes blink. A calm swept over me, my hands stopped shaking, and I sat still for probably 20 minutes, just peering out into the dark fields of kudzu surrounding me. I didn't know how that simple statement helped me, but I do know I felt less alone after that, and I believed God heard me and responded lovingly.

I restarted my truck, headed home, and enjoyed a good night's sleep. A couple months later, I met a woman online while nursing my office computer through the Y2K scare at midnight on January 1, 2000. Anne has been my stalwart companion, cheerleader, and companion for more than 25 years now. And my former gambling curse is an addiction of the distant past.

Times like that -- and there have been others -- are the main reason I'm still a believer, just trying to remain faithful in word and deed another day. I'm stacking up more good days than bad in that regard.

The life *applications* I've chosen of my faith's teaching have changed, however. Conservatives might call me a liberal, but that's okay if it means I'm more focused on how I can best translate love into action as a writer than on, say, singing praises to God all day long in praise and worship settings.

I've always likened God's love to my parents' love for me, and I've always felt Mom and Dad wouldn't have wanted me to spend all my time shouting praises to them instead of just living a positive life. I have a hunch that God wants more of me than that, as well. I think it's like He's saying, *"Take this love I've given you and do something grown-up with it. You and I are always good. No need for all the repetitive words and praises."*

In my writings, I've found a way to connect with people and to hopefully inspire them to vote for love rather than hate. In the stories I've told, I hope they can learn positive lessons from what love, beauty and tragedy can teach us, if we let them.

Oh, and about that job interview that launched this essay? I got that faculty slot. So, I must have passed muster okay.

I spent 17 enjoyable years at that California school, working alongside some fine colleagues and great students. I still stay in touch with many of them today.

Some of them still are listening to what I have to say today!

Writing a book leaves little time for loafing in retirement.
Jim Willis

45

Answering my own Question

I was talking with my older son recently, and he told me how he loves his career as a sales rep for a huge pharmaceutical firm, but that he's working hard to retire at 55. Maybe even sooner.

He will probably make it, because he is so successful, but he was talking to a dad who had just retired (a second time) at age 74. So I asked him, "And then, do what?"

"Then I do what I want to do and enjoy life, Dad," he responded.

"But I thought you were already doing that," I said.

"Hmmm," said he.

The long pause

That was followed by a long pause, as he thought about that question. A year later, I guess he's still thinking. I'm still waiting for his answer.

To me, that's a good thing. When to retire, and why you even *want to* are questions worth a lot of pondering before you actually pull the career plug. Because if you do it as early as my son wants to, you may have four decades left to fill with something as meaningful as work can be.

Otherwise that's a long time to watch the grass grow.

The career tree

I've had a trifurcated career in which all three branches have complemented each other. There were the ten years as a full-time journalist, followed by forty years as a college professor, and mixed into those four decades I authored seventeen books. I loved my career, and am still pruning the third branch of that tree as I work on a history of my Oklahoma hometown.

It took two swings at the bat to actually slide into retirement from my California university. I swung the first time in 2017, but the ball fell short of the cheap seats. I was back at work in 2018, happily so, until I found my workplace to be a different world even though I'd only been gone a year.

"We're so glad to have you back," was something I heard several times during my first few weeks. "Your experience and institutional knowledge will be invaluable to us and your young colleagues."

Oh really?

During faculty meetings, however, that sentiment seemed to translate as follows: My young colleagues would ask what I thought about proposed changes to my discipline's curriculum. They then tried valiantly to appear interested in my opinions. Who knows? Maybe some were. But then, when the voting came, they seemed to treat my advised with a grain of salt and voted on the issue the way they had already planned.

It was obvious my young friends were intent on doing what they wanted in order to show they were leading the department into a better future. So much for my experience. I probably did the same thing as a 30-something assistant professor in Boston, so I get it. Karma gets its revenge.

But it was enough to make me take the second swing at retirement in 2020. This time, I hit the ball out of the park. I was ready for the next game of life.

Now it's 2023, and I still miss teaching college kids. I miss seeing the excitement and passion of young minds. There were always enough of them to outweigh the others in my classroom who would rather be in Philadelphia.

A-g-e-i-s-m

I've missed it so much that I've tried to reinsert myself back into the academy's carousel a few times since 2020. I came close to being hired a couple times, but my age always kept the brass ring just out of reach. The professor *emeritus* title bestowed on me at retirement — the thing I was proud of (and still am) — became an apparent turnoff to younger faculties looking for younger candidates.

I can still recall a former dean telling me, when I tried to hire a 64-year-old talented journalist for the department, "Well, I think we'd rather have someone more at the start of their career than at the end of it. And, by the way, that's cheaper, too."

So, I've realized that if schools wince over someone who is 64, what chance does a guy in his mid-70s have? And, in truth, that realization has *liberated* me to focus more on my work itself than worrying about my marketability.

Working it out

I've been officially retired for five years now, and I think I've gotten the hang of it. I'm learning that the relevance I was so worried about is achievable by doing the work I love, and doing it on my own schedule. And I don't have to worry about:

1. Academic meetings that go nowhere and take hours getting there.
2. Cell phones in the classroom that waste my time, the students' time, and the money their parents paid to put them in the classroom.
3. Artificial intelligence programs writing the kids' papers and tricking out monitoring systems like Turnitin.com.

Who's not busy?

I can be as busy or as lazy as I want, and I've found both of those to be complementary.

I read and write a lot. I love writing for the site *Retrospect*, and I've just finished one 350-page memoir of a crucible period in my life, which followed my book, *Tinkertown*. I play my guitars daily and, since retirement, have recorded some 25 songs and uploaded them in videos to YouTube. And three years ago I started selling guitars downtown and have the only guitar shop in town.

When my self-directed career gets too busy, I put on my bathing suit (or not at night) and do laps in my backyard pool. I love spending glorious hangout time with my wife Anne who knows how to make me laugh. A lot. Or I just wrestle with my three dogs. (Oops...Anne tells me No. 4 will be here tomorrow.)

And, recently, I've even given myself permission to take naps.

About that talk

So now, after writing all this about retirement, I think I'll go have another talk with my son. If he hasn't come up with a good response to that retirement question I asked last year, maybe I can help him answer it now.

The Lion's energy of youth and the lion's heart of maturity.
Pixabay

46

We Lions in Winter

"*The more sand that has escaped through the hourglass of our life, the clearer we should see through it.*" -- Jean-Paul Sartre

As I thought about how to approach this prompt of *aging*, a moment in time from 1957 came flowing over me. I was in our family car with Mom, my sister C.J., and a couple neighborhood friends, and we were all headed to Oklahoma's big semi-centennial celebration in Oklahoma City.

Our state had just turned 50, which seemed so old to me then but now seems so young. Oklahoma was the 46th state to obtain statehood, beating out Arizona and New Mexico by five years, and Alaska and Hawaii by 52 years.

A child's worry

I was 11 in 1957 and, as we drove toward the celebration, I remember wondering whether I would still be alive when Oklahoma turned 100 in the year (gulp!) 2007. If I were, I thought, I would be 61 and so very old. I shuddered and put the thought out of my mind.

It would turn out that I *was* still alive in 2007, now sixteen years ago, and I don't feel all that old. Not only am I still alive today, but yesterday I completed a personal-best 18,140 steps on a 10,000-step daily regimen I began four years ago.

At the end of that feat, I wanted to turn to the 11-year-old Jimmy and say, "The future is not what it used to be, huh kid?"

Delaying tactics

I have done my best to put off feeling old for a lot of years now, and have pretty much succeeded. I waited until I was 74 to retire from college teaching, but I refuse to retire from writing and have written a couple books and a lot of *Retrospect* pieces since then.

I exercise now more than I have since college days, and I do it mostly to keep the inner dinosaur at bay. He's just going to have to wait for his day, and I guess I'll know when it's his turn.

A life of grace

Until then, I'll keep training my mind to stay active by writing, reading, and ... of course ... doing daily Wordle puzzles. As long as the light is on upstairs, I believe I can handle the body's eroding foundation downstairs.

In case any of this sounds a bit smug, I don't mean it to be. I am fully aware I am one of the lucky ones who has managed to escape debilitating illness, injury, and premature death, and I realize that comes by grace and not merit. I have lost count of my friends, loved ones, and classmates who have faced more hardships than I have.

Save for five heart stents and some skin cancer surgeries, I've had few health setbacks. To say I'm grateful is a gross understatement.

Finding the plusses

The upside of aging doesn't get talked about much, taking backseat to the often-heard laments like, "Old age is not for sissies." The past two or three years, however, have shown me there are a lot of positives to this business of ... maturity. Among those benefits are having time to reflect on what I've been too busy to enjoy, and chief among these enjoyments are the memories that make up my life ... so far.

Retirement has also stripped away most of my reasons for procrastinating about doing things I've always wanted to spend more time doing. Things like spending more quality time with the woman I've loved for so long, and more time with my guitar late at night in my blue-lit man cave. And, although it has been the substance of my career, I've spent more time writing and reading, just for the fun of it.

Living the dream

As I write this I'm sitting out on the patio with my English Setter Blue sprawled beside me on the lounge chair, and my Beagle/Foxhound George lying at my feet. We are all staring at something I've always wanted that lies just a few feet in front of us: a backyard lap pool. I eagerly await the 90+ degree days and the guilty pleasure of long daily swims as the dogs race me to the other end of the pool and back.

How bad can aging be if it allows you time to enjoy all this without worrying about what your work schedule says you should be doing instead, and indeed should have done by yesterday?

Surprises that sustain

I realize every day that growing older does not mean that more pleasant surprises don't lie ahead. I've experienced several recently, and I look forward to the next ones. I feel at one with Nick Nolte's character of Tom Wingo who, late in the film *Prince of Tides* muses, "It is the mystery of life that sustains me now."

And I am now old enough to understand and appreciate Albert Einstein's thought, "I live in that solitude which is painful in youth but delicious in the years of maturity."

It's a thought that would have made no sense to me on that summer day in Oklahoma, 1957. But now it means everything.

A watch tracks the shifting sands of time. But which way do they go?
Pixabay

47

Like a Circle in a Spiral

I was 16 when my Midwest City friend and classmate Ben Braswell passed, and I remember standing near his grave at the funeral on a day when the winds really did come sweeping down the plains of Oklahoma.

I was feeling very sad and very confused. I was in shock and already missed Ben. And it was the first time I remember thinking seriously about the thing we call *time*, how it related to Ben and me, and I had no answers. Ben had been so young, full of life, and was so much fun to be around.

He was always looking ahead. And then, in one unguarded moment on the highway, he wasn't. And that perplexed me.

A timely question

As the preacher was delivering the sermon (to Southern Baptist pastors, funerals are *always* a good time to deliver a sermon) I was thinking instead, "What should I make of Ben's death?" Does time just really stop, or is our definition of time just really wrong?

I knew I wasn't alone in my wonderings. To a teenager, life will go on forever. Time will go on forever. And when it doesn't, as it didn't for Ben, my friends and I asked,"What should we make of that?"

The stock answers (ie. *"God needed him there more than we need him here"*) may have worked for a short while, but they didn't work long. I guess because Ben was my friend, I couldn't let his passing go with such a quick fix.

On that particular November day, I did find myself wanting more of a reason that Ben's time was cut so short. The whole life he had ahead of him had just evaporated, all because of one moment in time. Absent an answer or even a framework for finding one, I finally let it go.

And yet, since I'm still writing about it six decades later, I guess I didn't.

Musical clues

That may be why songs that are *about* time have resonated with me over the years. There was Jim Croce's *Time in a Bottle*, the Beatles' *Yesterday*, Garrett Hedlund's *Timing is Everything*, Green Day's *Good Riddance* (aka *Time of your Life)*, and Paul Anka's *The Times of Your Life* (which became the theme song for Kodak commercials}. *Even the Bergmans' and* Legrand's *Windmills of Your Mind* deals with time and its riddles as it reflects, *"... Like a clock whose hands are sweeping past the minutes of its face ..."*

The fact there have been so many songs on this theme underscores how much importance we all attach to time. We equate it with life, and we feel life will be somehow be better if it lasts a long, long time. We feel a person is cheated if he or she passes before reaching that moving-target age where it seems okay to die.

A few songs have spoken to me, and the lyrics have helped lead me toward a peaceful cease-fire (if not a resolution itself) with my angst over the nature of time.

Time for young and old

A French songwriter, Charles Aznavour and his lyricist Herbert Kretzmer captured the young person's vague idea of time in the song, *Yesterday, When I was Young.* In it are phrases like, *"I teased at life as if it were a foolish game, the way the evening breeze may tease a candle flame."*

As I was singing and recording this song a few weeks ago, I realized that's exactly what I (and probably Ben) did when we were young. We did not take threats to life and time seriously until, one day, we realized we should have. After all, if the concluding lyrics to Aznavour's haunting song are true, *"...the time has come for me to pay for yesterday, when I was young."*

Time as circular

Still, knowing this doesn't really answer the question of how time should be regarded, or if there is a one-size-fits-all definition. Certainly the young among us view it differently than the old. Songwriter Joni Mitchell said as much in her song, *The Circle Game,* back in the 6os. Tracing the life of a young boy as he turned older, Mitchell reminded us that the young want time to speed up (*"words like, 'when you're older,' must appease him"*) but, as we grow older, the desire is to *"drag your feet to slow the circles down."*

Several songwriters have used the circle imagery when writing about time and its passing. Harry Chapin certainly did it when he came right out and named his song, *Circle*.

Right from the start, Chapin sings, *"All my life's a circle..."* Then he adds another element that most of us have wondered about when it comes to time: *"It seems like I've been here before; I can't remember when; But I have this funny feeling, that we'll all be together again"*

The thing about circles, of course, is they don't end. They just keep on going.

Johnny Cash, Waylon Jennings, Kris Kristofferson, and Willie Nelson (aka The Highwaymen), picked up on that circular element to the end of time, with their song, Highwayman. Each takes a whack at the concept of unbounded, circular time with his own verse. Cash wraps it up by musing he may become a highwayman again, *"... or I may simply be a single drop of rain .... but I will remain, and I'll be back again and again and again."*

Then, of course, there's Elton John's *The Circle of Life*. That link takes you to a spine-tingling interpretation of it by Alex Boye', with a few backup singers known as the Mormon Tabernacle Choir. Sir Elton's thoughts on time and life are on display with lyrics like, *"it moves us all to despair, hope, faith, and love ... till we find our place on this path unwinding, in the circle, the circle of life."*

Focusing the lens

When children are perplexed by reality, their parents will often counsel them that they will understand when they're older. That's been true about many things in my life, but not so much about understanding what to make of time. As an adult, I have continued to wonder: Should I fight for more of it, and feel sad for those who have dismounted Joni Mitchell's "painted ponies"? Or should I believe the departed have just entered another phase of time with its own colorful carousel?

At times, I think of what Harry Chapin wrote: *"No straight lines make up my life, and all my roads have bends; There's no clearcut beginning, and so far, no dead-ends."*

So, if that's true here, might it not be true where Ben Braswell is, too?

As a friend once noted in a spontaneous utterance the moment my father-in-law passed: *"His last breath here is his first breath there."*

I like that. It opens up a whole new world to ponder.

About the Author

Jim Willis is a veteran journalist, author, and professor emeritus at California's Azusa Pacific University. He has spent decades roaming the country and the world, writing about what he has done, witnessed, and learned. This is his 23rd published book. Most of his previous works have discussed the workings of journalism and media in society, although four were histories focused on the 1960s, and one was a history of his beloved Oklahoma Sooners football team in the 1990s, co-authored with a star lineman from that team. Jim grew up in Oklahoma where, he says, his heart will always lie. He graduated from OU and got his Ph.D. in Journalism from the University of Missouri. He is married to his musician wife, Anne Kindred Willis, and the couple live in Winchester, Kentucky with their half-dozen dogs and cats. They have six children and stepchildren. Jim says he will keep writing until the end. Both he and Anne are living lives of peace, hope, and love.

Jim Willis